So You Want to Teach?

A Guide to Teacher Certification

written by
Natalie Crittendon, M.Ed.

*Dedicated to every educator
who dares to dream, and
to those whose guidance
turns dreams into classrooms.*

SO YOU WANT TO TEACH?
A Guide To Teacher Certification

Written By
Natalie Crittendon, M.Ed.

Cover Designed By
Sun Child Wind Spirit

Proofread By
Mylia Tiye Mal Jaza

SO YOU WANT TO TEACH?
A Guide To Teacher Certification
Copyright © 2025, Natalie Crittendon
All Rights Reserved.

ISBN-13: 978-5810685272   ISBN-10: 2266966316

This literary art is a non-fiction work ideal for adults in the education profession. No part of this book may be reproduced or transmitted in any form or by any means (graphic, electronic, magnetic, photographic, or mechanical - including photocopying, recording, taping, or by any information storage/retrieval system) without the written permission of the compiling author. Post demise of author/publisher and self-publishing associate, then valid permission must be obtained from multiple immediate/major survivors of the author's family.

Author
Natalie Crittendon, M.Ed.
ntcrittendon@gmail.com

Self-Publishing Associate
Dr. Mary M. Jefferson
BePublished.Org - Chicago, IL
(972) 880-8316
www.bepublished.org

First Edition.
Printed in the United States of America.
Recycled Paper Encouraged.

Table of Contents

Introduction 9

References 163

Appendix 172

Section 1: Setting the Course

Chapter 1: The Crucial Role of Teacher Certification 19

Chapter 2: Knowing Your Why: Personal 31
    Motivation and Mindset

Section 2: Forging the Foundation

Chapter 3: Foundations First: Understanding Pedagogy 43

Chapter 4: Certification Requirements Demystified 54

Part 3: Mastery Through Experience

Chapter 5: Classroom Realities: The Student 66
    Teaching Experience

(more)

TOC *(cont'd)*

Part 4: Demonstrating Readiness

Chapter 6: State-by-State: Navigating Legal and 77
 Geographic Hurdles

Chapter 7: Building Your Teaching Portfolio 96

Part 5: From Candidate to Licensed Professional

Chapter 8: Beyond Certification: Lifelong 108
 Learning and Professional Development

Chapter 9: Technology, Tools, and Teacher 119
 Certification in the 21st Century

Chapter 10: Professional Attire 131

Part 6: Sustaining Excellence

Chapter 11: Certified and Empowered: Owning Your 139
 Role as a Professional Educator

Conclusion: Role as a Professional Educator 150
 Building a Successful Teaching Career: Certification
 and Professional Growth

(###)

Introduction
Launching the Path to Transformational Teaching

> "Education is not preparation for life; education is life itself."
> — John Dewey

The desire to be a teacher has always been something I wanted to accomplish. From the early days of my childhood one of the games I played with my peers is the game of "School". We would seat the dolls in perfect rows and begin to teach our pretend students all of the wonderful things that our teachers had taught us in my school. Teachers influence all that we do, and I knew that I would one day teach. The burning desire to be a professional educator has always been a part of me. As an undergrad I chose to major in education, and I have remained in the field for 30 years. As we begin this journey of seeking teacher certification, my desire is that you develop that same passion for becoming a certified educator that began in me years ago.

From the first page of this book, I want to invite you into one of the most consequential professions in human history. Teaching doesn't just transfer knowledge — it shapes the thinkers, leaders, and innovators of tomorrow. And at the heart of every great teacher stands a foundation of professional preparation, deep understanding, and ethical responsibility. That foundation? Teacher certification.

By learning not only *what* to teach but *how* to teach, and by earning the legitimate credentials that confirm your readiness, certification signals a promise: a commitment to excellence, to equity, and to impact. Whether you dream of igniting a lifelong love of reading in kindergartners or equipping high school students to tackle civic challenges, your role is pivotal, and teacher certification is the cornerstone that empowers you to fulfill that role with integrity, skill, and confidence.

Why Teacher Certification Matters

In today's world, children face more complexity than ever: a digital influx of information, widening achievement disparities, cultural heterogeneity within classrooms, and rapidly shifting workforce demands. Against this backdrop, the days of learning to "just wing it" in front of students are over. Community expectations — of students, families, and society — are crystal clear: Our educators must be expertly prepared.

Consider these truths:

- **Learning science matters.** Research shows how the brain acquires and retains knowledge, but only when teachers understand and apply these insights can learning be truly optimized.

- **Diverse classrooms require cultural competency.** Today's teachers must navigate language barriers, culturally reflective pedagogy, and equity-centered practices.

- **Rigorous academic standards demand mastery.** A teacher must teach content deeply, convey standards, and prepare students for advanced studies and the workforce.

Teacher certification is more than paperwork — it is an attestation: *"I am equipped."* It's a statement to students, parents, colleagues, and yourself that you are ready to guide the next generation.

A Promise to Students and Communities

> "To teach is to touch a life forever."
> — Unknown

When a teacher enters a classroom, they enter a space of impact. Missed or misinformed teaching can shape a child's self-concept and potential. When things are taught incorrectly to students it takes years to reverse the damage. Conversely, skilled and prepared teachers inspire confidence, perseverance, and curiosity. Certification instills a deep sense of responsibility — understanding that a teacher's choices and practices echo far beyond the classroom walls.

Communities, too, place immense trust in educators. Families depend on schools to help children develop intellectually, emotionally, and ethically. Earning a certification signals that you take that trust seriously — and that you're accountable. You haven't simply declared your intent to teach; you've demonstrated it, evidenced through academic preparation, supervised practice, ethical vetting, and formal assessment.

When Aspiration Meets Preparation

> "The mediocre teacher tells. The good teacher explains. The superior teacher demonstrates. The great teacher inspires."
> — William Arthur Ward

Aspiring teachers often begin with noble intentions — and the best of intentions. But without guidance, those good intentions can falter. Certification programs serve as carefully designed bridges:

1. **Knowledge of Learners and Learning** – Understanding developmental stages, learning styles, and neurodiversity, and learning how to meet learners' individual needs.

2. **Content Expertise** – A teacher of math needs to *know* math; a history teacher needs historical depth and know the correct historical facts.

3. **Pedagogical Skill** – Strategies for instruction, classroom management, literacy, technology integration, and critical inquiry.

4. **Applied Experience** – Intentional, supervised practicum where you test, reflect, and grow.

5. **Ethical Preparation** – Learning your obligations, responsibilities, and professional boundaries.

Certification programs link these phases into a coherent journey. You move from learner to doer, to leader. You transform your passion into informed instruction. You learn not just to teach, but how to teach effectively.

Excellence That Can Be Measured, Validated, and Improved

Certification isn't meant to stifle individuality — it standardizes excellence. It establishes clear expectations and aligns professionals around shared principles. When you earn a certificate, it means you've:

- Met a rigorous set of state-defined benchmarks
- Passed knowledge and skills-based exams

- Completed supervised, real-world classroom practice
- Understood professional norms including inclusivity, confidentiality, and reflective practice

But beyond the initial licensing, certification also serves as a springboard for ongoing learning. In many states teachers must renew their licenses periodically. This perpetual cycle ensures no teacher remains stagnant — each is compelled to stay current with research, diversify methodologies, and innovate in instruction.

Your Role, Your Journey

A teacher's career is a journey of constant impact and iteration. This book is your companion on that journey — from aspiring educator to certified professional to reflective practitioner.

Here's how the chapters unfold:

- **Part 1: Setting the Course**
  Mapping your path — choosing grade levels, subjects, and pathways (traditional vs. alternative). Understanding how states categorize teachers and what that means for your goals.

- **Part 2: Forging the Foundation**
  Earning your degree, entering an approved educator preparation program, and meeting the unique needs of multilingual and diverse classrooms through standards-aligned coursework.

- **Part 3: Mastery Through Experience**
  Learning in practice — fieldwork, observation, clinical teaching,

and self-reflection. These sections describe how each moment in the classroom transforms your potential into effectiveness.

- **Part 4: Demonstrating Readiness**
Preparing for and passing the various state certification exams — Content, Professional Pedagogy and Responsibility (PPR), and STR- Science of Teaching Reading (where applicable). Realistic timelines, study strategies, and support systems laid out clearly to keep you advancing.

- **Part 5: From Candidate to Licensed Professional**
Navigating your states Education and Career Opportunities System (ECOS) portal, submitting transcripts, undergoing fingerprinting, preparing a competitive application. This section ensures administrative hurdles don't hold you back.

- **Part 6: Sustaining Excellence**
Resume creation, interviewing, job-search strategies using region service centers and district platforms. Mentoring, induction programs, and how to enter your first classroom with confidence. Maintaining your certification through ongoing learning, professional development (CPE hours), and preparing for advancement. Each renewal cycle is described as a new opportunity for growth, not merely an obligation.

Voices of Endorsement

Throughout the book, I'll bring in voices like yours — teachers who began from uncertainty and found clarity, readiness, and impact through certification. But also voices of famed educators whom history has recognized:

> "The highest result of education is tolerance."
> — Helen Keller

> "We do not learn from experience...we learn from reflecting on experience."
> — John Dewey

> "It is the supreme art of the teacher to awaken joy in creative expression and knowledge."
> — Albert Einstein

> "Good teaching is more a giving of right questions than a giving of right answers."
> — Josef Albers

Each quote reinforces that teaching is much more than content delivery. It is reflection, artistry, empathy, rigor, and curiosity — all tied together by a framework of standards and preparation that ensures educators are equipped to nurture those qualities in students.

Certification as a Rite of Passage

Certification isn't an end — it's a powerful rite of passage. By completing it, you signal:

- *Academic* readiness
- *Supervised* preparation
- *Ethical* awareness
- *Reflective* professionalism
- *Ongoing* growth

That credential opens doors in districts, signals credibility, and gives you the tools to craft learning environments that are dynamic, thoughtful, and student-centered. Once certified, you stand within a professional community — a community committed to excellence in education.

The Soil for Lifelong Growth

Imagine your certification not as a capstone, but as fertile soil. Once you've planted the seeds:

- Your teaching blossoms with confidence and insight.
- Your evaluations become opportunities for self-discovery rather than stress.
- Your students thrive under expert guidance.
- Your community knows teaching is more than a job — it's a profession deserving of respect.

Every professional gathering you attend, every workshop you complete, every advanced certification you pursue — these expand what began the day you earned your initial credential.

What Comes Next

So now, in your hands, you hold more than a guide. You hold the map along with turn-by-turn instructions resource, and ally. You're not alone in the journey. The book will walk you the steps with clarity, support, and practical tools.

Paired with the downloadable checklist and printable coaching guide we've prepared, you now have both macro and micro tools: the big-picture pathway and the day-to-day details.

This introduction is your invitation — yes, invitation — to engage fully. You'll encounter inspiring anecdotes, proven strategies, sample documents, exercises, and timelines. You'll dig into real coaching conversations, frequent pitfalls, and moments of celebration.

Invitation to the Chapter Ahead

As you turn the page into Chapter 1, ask yourself:

- What level and subject area ignite your passion?
- What's your current confidence level with teaching fundamentals?

- What kind of support do you need: peer, mentor, institution?
- What's the one obstacle that feels most daunting — and how might clearing it unlock a full cascade of forward movement?

This isn't a book of theory — this is a playbook. When folded into your life, certification becomes more than status; it becomes a dynamic process that shapes you as an educator, crafts your practice, and sends ripples through countless lives.

A Final Thought

> "It takes a big heart to shape little minds."
> — Anonymous

Look in the mirror. That heart is there. Certification helps you channel it with knowledge, skill, and ethics. You're not just teaching — you're building, transforming, and empowering. Certification confirms that mission and powers your next step.

So you want to teach. Let's begin!

Chapter 1:
The Crucial Role of Teacher Certification

> "Better than a thousand days of diligent study is one day with a great teacher." – Japanese proverb

Have you ever wondered what truly separates someone who claims to teach from a teacher who is prepared, skilled, and trusted? As a campus administrator I have had certified and non-certified teachers in the schools that I lead. I had novice teachers seeking certification but did not take it seriously. Oftentimes they missed certification program deadlines which had a great impact on their personal finances. The need for certification is crucial.

Imagine walking into a classroom where the person standing in front of you hasn't had any formal training or assessment how confident would you feel about the lessons, the safety, and the fairness of that environment? Many people consider teaching simply as sharing knowledge, but it's so much more than that. Being an effective educator means mastering not only the subject matter but also the art of guiding diverse learners, managing classrooms, and upholding ethical responsibilities.

Becoming a certified teacher is a key part of this process. It's not just a piece of paper; certification is a carefully designed system meant to ensure teachers meet professional standards, protect students, and support educators' growth over time. Whether you're just starting out, thinking about changing careers, or coming from another country, understanding how teacher certification works is essential. This chapter will explain why certification matters, what it involves, and the challenges you might face along the way. It's your roadmap to navigating the path toward becoming a quality certified, respected, and successful educator.

The Necessity of Teacher Certification

So you want to teach? Teaching certification acts as the formal threshold that distinguishes qualified educators from those who may lack the necessary preparation or commitment to high professional standards. Certification establishes a requirement that aspiring teachers prove their readiness to work with young people by completing accredited education programs, passing required exams, and meeting ethical guidelines. These checks are vital in creating a clear line between individuals who are professionally equipped to shape student lives and those who are not.

Certification ensures teaching quality by demanding evidence of mastery in pedagogy, subject knowledge, and classroom management. In most certification pathways, candidates must complete coursework that covers child development, teaching strategies, and curriculum planning. For example, a high school math teacher is typically required to have a degree in mathematics along with teacher preparation training. In addition, passing rigorous state exams in content knowledge and pedagogical practice is a universal requirement. This is similar to the process in other fields such as medicine, where doctors must demonstrate expertise before earning a license to practice. Certification also often includes a supervised teaching component, such as student teaching or internships, where future teachers demonstrate their abilities in real classrooms under the guidance of experienced mentors. These layers of assessment serve as quality control, making sure teachers understand both what they teach and how to teach it effectively.

Students benefit directly from these certification standards, which constitute the minimal requirements of a professional educator. By restricting classroom entry to those who meet ethical and professional benchmarks, certification systems help protect students from exposure to unqualified or potentially harmful adults. Required background checks are a prime example, every certified teacher must pass a criminal history screening before working in a school. In addition to safety, students benefit when teachers are trained to manage behavior, support learning differences, and foster a positive classroom culture. Ethics training, which is integral to the certification process, teaches new educators about their responsibility to nurture the democratic principles of equality and fairness, to avoid favoritism, and to protect students from harm or embarrassment (National Education Association, 2020). This ethical grounding ensures all students are treated with respect, regardless of background or ability, and that teachers know how to respond if they witness improper conduct among colleagues or students (Upholding Professional Ethics in Education for Fairness, 2024).

Certification is not just a requirement for individual teachers, it elevates the profession as a whole. By establishing professional benchmarks, certification aligns teaching with other respected fields that require licensure, such as engineering, nursing, or law. Each step in the certification process, academic training, practical teaching, ethical standards, sends a message that teaching is both a science and an art, deserving of the same seriousness as other professions that directly influence public well-being. For example, the NEA's Code of Ethics demands that teachers maintain high standards, reveal no false qualifications, and refrain from misrepresenting their credentials (National Education Association, 2020). These standards help ensure the teaching workforce is held in high esteem, reinforcing public trust and attracting capable, dedicated individuals into the field.

Community trust in schools and teachers often centers on the reassurance that those entrusted with students' education are qualified and accountable. Certification signals to parents and guardians that their children are in the care of professionals who have met recognized standards. This public assurance is further reinforced through systems of continuing education and ongoing evaluation. Certification is not usually a one-time process, teachers are required to update their credentials, participate in professional development, and, in many cases, periodically renew their certification to remain current with evolving educational best practices (Upholding Professional Ethics in Education for Fairness, 2024). This continuous oversight not only keeps teachers up to date but also maintains trust in an ever-changing educational landscape.

Accountability mechanisms built into certification help to foster community confidence. Should a certified teacher violate ethical codes or fail to meet standards, there is a clear process for disciplinary action, including the loss of certification if warranted (National Education Association, 2020). This transparency allows the public to see that educators are held to account for their actions, further strengthening the credibility of the teaching profession.

Professional certification also reflects legal requirements and employment standards, which govern who may teach and set the groundwork for fairness and quality in schools. These requirements will be explored further in the context of educational law, highlighting the close connection between certification, professional expectations, and students' right to quality instruction.

Legal and Career Implications of Certification

Across the United States, state laws make teacher certification a basic legal requirement for most public school teaching positions. Every state has its own certification process run by agencies or boards that set standards for entry. For example, Texas law clearly lays out the expectation for any person applying for a teaching role at a public school (EDUCATION CODE CHAPTER 21.

EDUCATORS, 2017). Applicants are required to submit affidavits confirming they have not engaged in inappropriate relationships with students, and the state board is responsible for checking that all applicants meet rigorous professional standards. If a school hires someone who is not properly certified, not only does the school risk penalties, but the teacher can be terminated from employment if the certification requirements are not met . In these cases, the lack of certification is grounds for immediate dismissal and the employee is often ineligible for appeal. This legal foundation exists across most states, ensuring that only well-prepared professionals are entrusted with classroom responsibilities. Considering this, we see that the very allowance of temporary certifications compromise the mandates.

These certification rules have practical implications for student safety and well-being. Certification ensures that teachers have received adequate preparation, know how to handle the ethical complexities of their role, and can create a productive and safe learning environment.

For example, the pre-employment affidavit requirement in Texas directly protects students by screening out individuals who have been charged or convicted of inappropriate conduct, demonstrating how certification processes go beyond academic qualifications to address safety and integrity (EDUCATION CODE CHAPTER 21. EDUCATORS, 2017). School districts use certification as a safeguard; it's a clear signal that a teacher is accountable to recognized standards and ongoing professional development.

Certified teachers also enjoy a range of career benefits and advantages compared to uncertified colleagues. Schools and districts typically list certification as a minimum qualification in job postings — being certified is often non-negotiable, especially in states with strict oversight. For example, district job listings for classroom teachers nearly always state, "Valid state teaching certification required." Many schools will not even consider uncertified candidates for permanent teaching roles; instead, those without certification find work as substitutes or in paraprofessional positions, which offer far less pay and stability. Certified teachers qualify for comprehensive benefits packages that include health insurance, retirement plans, paid leave, and even loan forgiveness programs — offerings often unavailable to non-certified staff (Job & Career Security | NEA, n.d.).

Salary differences are one of the most visible advantages. According to data from multiple states, certified teachers earn thousands of dollars more per year compared to paraprofessionals or substitute teachers. In some cases, long-term substitute teachers earn as much as 40% less than their certified counterparts in permanent positions. School districts, in order to attract and retain highly qualified staff, build their salary schedules around certification levels. Some offer additional pay bumps for advanced certification or for earning specialized credentials, such as bilingual or special education endorsements.

Certification is directly tied to job security and opportunities for advancement. Certified teachers typically enter into annual or multi-year contracts and often receive union protection, ensuring due process in the case of layoffs or other employment disputes (Job & Career Security | NEA, n.d.). If a teacher must renew, extend, or validate their certificate, there are clear procedures and safeguards to help maintain employment during lapses, provided the teacher acts in good faith and communicates proactively (EDUCATION CODE CHAPTER 21. EDUCATORS, 2017). By contrast, uncertified staff usually work at-will, and have little to no job protection and are the first to be let go during staffing reductions.

Certified teachers are also the only candidates eligible for many leadership roles in schools. Positions like instructional coach, department head, or curriculum coordinator explicitly require current teaching certification. School policies may even stipulate that only certified staff can mentor new teachers, serve on key committees, or apply for grant-funded projects aimed at professional development. As teachers gain experience, additional certification or advanced degrees open doors to administrative and district-level leadership. These pathways are visible in large districts where teacher leaders, literacy specialists, and technology integrationists step into formalized roles with higher pay and more influence over school policy.

School accreditation is deeply connected to the certification status of a teaching staff. Accrediting bodies look for evidence that a school employs only certified teachers as part of their standards review. If a district fails to maintain this requirement, it risks its accreditation, which can affect funding, student transfers, and community reputation. Because of this, districts prioritize certified teachers at every step of hiring and contract renewal.

For individuals considering a teaching career, certification is not only a legal hurdle but a gateway to a rewarding and secure professional life. It brings higher earning potential, better benefits, clearer paths for advancement, and protection from unpredictable employment practices, all while maintaining the standards that protect students and school communities (Job & Career Security | NEA, n.d.; EDUCATION CODE CHAPTER 21. EDUCATORS, 2017).

Navigating the Certification Process

The path to becoming a certified teacher begins with education. Most states expect future teachers to hold at least a bachelor's degree from an accredited college or university.

Undergraduate programs in education often include a mixture of general coursework, content area classes, and pedagogy. Students majoring in areas like math or English take core courses in their subject along with teacher preparation coursework. Coursework in pedagogy covers topics such as teaching strategies, classroom management, educational psychology, and serving learners with special needs (Certified vs Non-Certified Teacher - Main Difference in 2025 | Teachers of Tomorrow, 2025). As part of the journey, future teachers must complete assigned hours observing classrooms and participating in early field experiences. These activities help aspiring educators connect theory to real classroom situations and build foundational skills.

Standardized examinations play a crucial role in certification. Aspiring teachers often take general knowledge tests and subject-specific exams. For example, many states require the Praxis Core Academic Skills for Educators exam that covers reading, writing, and math. Subject area exams evaluate a candidate's depth of knowledge in the field they plan to teach, such as social studies or biology (Certified vs Non-Certified Teacher - Main Difference in 2025 | Teachers of Tomorrow, 2025). Some states also administer tests on professional practices and pedagogy, making sure teachers can translate subject expertise into effective teaching. Test preparation becomes a regular part of the certification process. Candidates review sample questions, practice timing, and identify weak areas. Test retakes are common and can extend the timeline, especially if a candidate needs to prepare for specialized topics, such as teaching students with disabilities or English language learners.

Every route to certification includes practical teaching experience. Most commonly, this takes the form of student teaching, an intensive internship that places an aspiring teacher in a real classroom under the guidance of a mentor teacher. Student teaching often spans a full semester and includes lesson planning, instruction, classroom management, and grading. A typical week involves co-teaching with the mentor, gradually taking on full teaching responsibilities, and receiving feedback from both university supervisors and classroom mentors. Full-time teaching during this period introduces aspiring educators to the daily realities of lesson delivery, responding to diverse learning needs, and managing classroom dynamics (Bowen & Williams, 2024). These experiences ensure that new teachers are classroom-ready before earning certification.

Different certification pathways provide flexibility for diverse candidates. Traditional certification usually involves a four-year bachelor's degree in education, followed by exams and a semester of student teaching (Certified vs Non-Certified Teacher - Main Difference in 2025 | Teachers of Tomorrow, 2025; Bowen & Williams, 2024). In contrast, alternative certification programs target career changers or mid-career professionals who already have a degree in another field. These programs may be offered as graduate-level courses or as intensive short-term workshops. Typical alternative pathways allow candidates to work as teachers of record while completing certification requirements in the evenings or on weekends. The alternative route compresses coursework, exam preparation, and student teaching into a one- to two-year period, instead of the traditional four years (Bowen & Williams, 2024). Some programs allow participants to complete requirements while earning a master's degree. State requirements influence the pace of each pathway. Some states require two years of classroom experience in addition to coursework and exams, while others approve certification after one year if all components are completed successfully.

Challenges appear at every stage. Standardized testing requirements can be difficult, especially for individuals re-entering school after years away from formal education. Every exam demands content review, test-taking strategy practice, and sometimes multiple attempts for passing scores. Practical teaching places candidates in unfamiliar school settings and demands long hours. Balancing coursework, lesson planning, and classroom responsibilities can become stressful. Many alternative certification candidates must juggle full-time employment, family obligations, and evening coursework. Weekly calendars fill quickly with teaching plus seminars, assignments, and exam preparation (Bowen & Williams, 2024).

Misconceptions about certification often led to confusion and wasted effort. For example, some believe that subject matter expertise alone is enough, but all states require demonstration of pedagogical skills through coursework, exams, and student teaching or internships. Others may underestimate the time required, overlooking state-specific requirements for coursework hours and field experiences. Online or accelerated programs still demand rigorous study and practical experience; no simple shortcut exists. On-the-job learning in alternative programs is valuable, but does not eliminate the need for formal assessment and hands-on experience in a supervised setting (Certified vs Non-Certified Teacher - Main Difference in 2025 | Teachers of Tomorrow, 2025).

A practical week for a teacher preparation candidate can include daytime hours in a classroom, evening coursework, weekly lesson planning, and regular progress meetings with supervisors. Effective time management brings structure, but the process remains demanding. Those who stay committed, using detailed schedules and seeking support from mentors, progress steadily toward certification. The journey requires persistence, flexibility, and a willingness to continually adapt and learn from experience (Bowen & Williams, 2024).

Bringing It All Together

Now that we understand why teacher certification is essential for maintaining quality education, protecting students, and advancing careers, we can approach the process with confidence and clarity. Whether you are just starting out, changing careers, preparing for exams, or new to the

U.S. system, knowing the steps ahead reduce uncertainty and keeps you focused on your goals. By staying committed to each stage, from coursework to testing to practical experience, you build the skills and credentials needed to become a trusted, certified, and effective educator. Remember, the path may have challenges, but it also opens doors to meaningful work, job security, and professional growth. With clear guidance and determination, you are well on your way to joining a respected profession that makes a real difference in students' lives every day.

Whenever you enter any new field you must always know why you are choosing to teach. This is not just a career that you can enter and not know why. Are you wanting to teach because you want to make a difference in the lives of children? Do you desire to teach because you want to emulate a teacher that greatly impacted your life? As we progress through this journey of teaching certification you must begin to seek and understand your "WHY". As we move forward the next chapter start thinking about the following: "Why do you want to become a teacher?" In chapter 2 we will delve into personal motivation and mindset.

Chapter 2:
Knowing Your Why: Personal Motivation and Mindset

The Teacher's Mindset: Foundations for Aspiring Educators

When I entered the field of education I was always asked, "Why do you want to teach?" When I was presented with this question it through me off. As I thought of my response I realized that I have always wanted to be a teacher. I have been a teacher all of my life in my heart. You must ask yourself this critical question. Your why is the driver to the reason you are entering this profession. By the close of this chapter my desire is that you can answer the question, "What is your why?" with clarity. Below is a scenario that one of my teachers that was in a teacher certification program experienced. The feelings of this young lady are real and this may become a feeling you may experience as you go through your certification journey. So you want to teach? Why?

"I don't know if I can do this," Tiffney whispered to herself as she stared at the mountain of reading assignments and lesson plans stacked on her desk. She had dreamed of becoming a teacher for years, but now that she was deep into the certification process, doubt crept in. Balancing coursework, exams, and classroom experiences felt overwhelming. Was her motivation strong enough to carry her through?

For many aspiring teachers like Tiffney, the path to certification is more than just checking boxes or passing test, it's about holding onto a deeper reason for stepping into the classroom in the first place. The challenges they face aren't just about mastering content; they test their patience, resilience, and belief in their own growth. Understanding what fuels that inner drive and learning how to navigate moments of self-doubt can make all the difference.

This chapter explores the mindset that shapes successful teachers from the very beginning such as why they choose this path beyond financial rewards, how they build strength when facing setbacks, and the practical steps they take to keep growing. Whether you're switching careers, preparing for your first teaching job, or simply wondering what it takes to stay committed, these insights offer a foundation to help you move forward with confidence.

Purpose Over Paycheck: The Teacher's Calling

Most successful teachers pursue certification for reasons deeper than a paycheck. On a side note: If you are looking for summers off I am sad to say that your summers will be filled with professional development. This is what makes the difference between average teachers and great teachers. Their motivation often begins with the desire to make a lasting impact on students' lives, extending beyond classroom walls. Teachers know that their influence shapes how students think, feel, and interact with the world. For example, a middle school teacher might design group projects that encourage respectful debate and cooperation, helping students see the value of multiple viewpoints. When a teacher encourages a shy student to share their ideas during a class discussion, this small encouragement can build the student's confidence for years to come. Teachers also nurture curiosity. Introducing a hands-on science experiment or a creative writing challenge sparks wonder and encourages students to ask bold questions, which can lead to independent learning far beyond specific lessons.

Critical thinking remains one of the most valuable skills teachers can foster. By challenging students to analyze information, compare sources, and defend opinions through evidence, teachers give students tools to navigate an information-rich world. Picture an elementary teacher guiding students through a news article, prompting them to separate fact from opinion and supporting them as they question the material. These moments help young people grow into adults who can make informed decisions. Teachers also see how their work ripples through entire communities. A passionate social studies teacher might partner with local organizations for service projects, or a math teacher could mentor students in after-school STEM clubs, sparking broader commitments to community improvement. Every time a teacher helps a student overcome personal or academic obstacles, they invest in building stronger, more resilient neighborhoods, ultimately contributing to social change.

Teachers often report that their drive springs from inherent, deeply fulfilling rewards. The joy of seeing a struggling reader finally finish a book or the excitement on a student's face when they solve a difficult problem are powerful motivators. These moments create a sense of pride that isn't tied to test scores or performance bonuses. According to current research, educators who focus on fostering intrinsic motivation in classrooms often see meaningful student growth and increased satisfaction in their profession (Breisacher, 2024). For many teachers, something as simple as a heartfelt thank-you note from a former student validates years of effort. Your return on investment you may not see for several years but when you get your ROI it is a feeling that is filled with pride and love for the student.

Professional growth is another central, internal reward. Teachers must adapt to students with different learning needs, backgrounds, and abilities. When a teacher successfully reaches a student who previously seemed disengaged, perhaps by adapting their teaching style or integrating a student's cultural interests into lessons, it often feels as meaningful as a pay raise. Mastery of new teaching techniques or technology brings its own kind of satisfaction. For example, when a teacher learns to use interactive whiteboards and sees student engagement soar, this sense of accomplishment reinforces their choice to stick with teaching, especially during demanding periods.

These intrinsic rewards play a critical role in helping teachers persist through the long and sometimes difficult pathway to certification. Teachers often encounter rigorous course loads, exam pressures, and challenging practicum assignments. Strong internal motivation, such as the desire to see children thrive, helps them stay focused and resilient. Research highlights how teachers' deep engagement and joy in their craft drive them through certification, guiding them to reflect on their learning and maintain perseverance even when external rewards are limited (Bardach & Klassen 2021).

Long-term commitment also helps teachers turn professional challenges into opportunities for personal growth. Certification requires dedication, as teachers must continually refine their practice and accept feedback on their teaching. When a teacher confronts a tough classroom situation, like managing disruptive behavior or supporting students with trauma, commitment drives them to seek creative solutions rather than give up. Setting personal goals, such as becoming a mentor, leading curricular teams, or advocating for educational equity, also connects individual ambitions to broader educational missions. Teachers committed to these goals often contribute to school cultures that value lifelong learning, inclusion, and community support.

Staying committed isn't just about completing coursework or passing exams. Teachers draw strength from their underlying motivations and values. They see daily progress in students, such as a child overcoming anxiety to present in front of the class, a team winning a state science competition, or a classroom community helping a new student feel welcome, as proof that their impact matters. These experiences affirm their role and renew their commitment, helping them weather setbacks like policy changes or classroom disruptions. A teacher's sense of purpose, grounded in the desire to inspire and nurture, is what elevates certification from a requirement to a meaningful milestone on a lifelong journey.

In the end, it is these foundational motivations like the desire to make a lasting difference, take pride in hard-won successes, and commit fully to the educational mission that not only draw teachers to certification but sustain them through every challenge they encounter on the path to becoming outstanding educators (Bardach & Klassen 2021).

Navigating Doubt and Foundational Mindset Skills

Facing the challenges of teacher certification often brings moments of self-doubt, especially when balancing coursework, exams, and unfamiliar classroom situations. Building self-belief is a dynamic process, and the right strategies can help keep confidence steady even when doubts start to overwhelm. One practical method is using positive self-talk in the heat of a stressful situation. For example, when preparing for a crucial assessment or facing difficult exam content, telling yourself, "I have worked hard, and I am capable," helps counter negative thoughts. Repeating phrases like, "Mistakes mean I'm learning," or "Effort leads to progress," plants seeds of self-confidence and creates a buffer during tense moments. These phrases can be written on sticky notes and posted near a study area or recited out loud before walking into an exam. The goal is to gradually shift internal dialogue to support effort and persistence rather than focusing on fear.

Self-doubt is not a sign of weakness; it's a natural byproduct of trying something new and challenging. It's helpful to recognize and accept that everyone experiences it, especially when navigating high-stakes requirements. By acknowledging doubt as a sign that you are stepping outside your comfort zone, it becomes easier to pause, take stock of your emotions, and then choose a constructive response. A growth-oriented mindset is fueled by these very moments. Mindset theory emphasizes that how you interpret setbacks shapes your future actions (Yeager & Dweck, 2020): seeing struggles as evidence that you are building new skills reframes the narrative from "I'm not good enough," to "I am still learning." For example, after receiving a disappointing score on a practice test, instead of focusing on failure, you might review feedback and identify one or two specific areas to improve. This is a practice that gradually builds both skill and self-assurance.

Journaling provides a powerful way to process challenging experiences and reinforce an adaptive mindset. Candidates can use a three-step journaling exercise at the end of each week. First, write about one challenging moment: What happened, and how did you feel? Second, reflect on how you responded and what beliefs shaped your actions. Third, note what you learned and what you would try next time. For instance, a candidate struggling with classroom management in their student teaching placement might reflect on the specific challenges, acknowledge what strategies succeeded or fell short, and then commit to trying a new classroom routine the following week. Over time, this practice strengthens the connection between reflection, learning, and forward movement (Ba et al., 2025).

Setting specific, manageable goals is another direct way to overcome the inertia caused by doubt. Rather than aiming to "master all teaching material," set daily or weekly objectives such as "read one chapter," "complete two lesson plans," or "ask my mentor one question about assessment." Breaking large tasks into bite-sized, achievable steps provides a sense of accomplishment, which fuels motivation and helps keep momentum steady. Using a simple goal-setting table, candidates can map progress each week and celebrate milestones along the way.

Feedback and Stress Management for Teacher Success

Psychological barriers often make feedback difficult for aspiring teachers. When receiving critique, the brain may react defensively. A comment on a lesson plan can feel like a threat to your capabilities. This emotional response is natural, but learning to recognize it is the key to transforming feedback into growth. Mindfulness training and self-efficacy, often discussed as central to teacher well-being, play a critical role here (Flook et al., 2013). Approaching feedback as data rather than a judgment can help build resilience and support a growth mindset, enabling you to turn initial discomfort into meaningful action. Below are recommendations for ways to positively handle the stress that you will encounter as you navigate your certification journey:

The Feedback Journal

Purpose: Create a structured, private space to process and implement critique.

Implementation Steps:

1. After each feedback session, record the main points given — both strengths and areas for growth.
2. Reflect on your immediate reaction and note it honestly.
3. Identify one concrete step you can try based on the critique.
4. Track your attempts and outcomes over the next few days.
5. At the end of the week, review your notes to spot progress or patterns.

Success Indicators:
You process feedback objectively, see trends in strengths and

growth areas, and reduce emotional reactivity over time.

Common Challenges & Solutions:
Some feel resistance writing about negative feedback. Reframe this as collecting useful information for self-improvement. If overwhelmed, break your reflection into two short sessions.

The Growth Grid

Purpose: Visualize feedback trends and growth over time.
Implementation Steps:
1. Draw a simple two-column table: "Feedback Theme" and "Action/Progress."
2. Each time you get feedback (e.g., lesson pacing, clarity, student engagement), log the theme in the first column.
3. In the second column, briefly describe your response — what you tried and what changed.
4. Review the grid monthly for recurring patterns and improvements.

Success Indicators:
You can point to specific areas where you've improved and recall what strategies helped, making feedback less overwhelming and more actionable.

Common Challenges & Solutions:
If patterns are hard to spot, ask a peer or mentor to review your grid with you. If you receive conflicting feedback from different evaluators, log both perspectives and note which responses produced better results.

The Response Protocol

Purpose: Maintain professionalism and use evaluations as springboards for growth.

Implementation Steps:

1. When receiving feedback, listen silently and take notes.
2. Thank the giver with a simple phrase ("Thank you for your input — I appreciate it").
3. Ask clarifying questions if unsure about a point ("Can you show me an example from today's lesson?").
4. State one action you'll take: "I'll try that strategy in tomorrow's warm-up activity."
5. Afterward, jot down how you felt and what you learned.

Success Indicators:
You feel more confident and less defensive during feedback sessions, and evaluators note your openness.

Common Challenges & Solutions:
If you freeze during feedback, practice the protocol with a friend or record yourself rehearsing professional responses.

In real certification scenarios, a career changer may receive critique on their first lesson structure — applying the Response Protocol can help them remain composed, while the Growth Grid shows their steady adjustment to classroom timing.

5-5-5 Grounding Technique

Purpose: Reduce pre-observation anxiety and refocus rapidly.

Implementation Steps:
1. Sit comfortably. Inhale for five seconds, hold for five seconds, exhale for five seconds.
2. Name five things you can see, four you can touch, three you can hear, two you can smell, one you can taste.
3. Repeat the breathing cycle twice.

Success Metrics:
You notice your heart rate slows and your focus on immediate tasks increases; observer feedback highlights your calm presence.

Adaptation:
For high stress, shorten the technique to just the breathing cycle. Integrate before every observation or challenging meeting.

Integration:
Set a phone reminder for 10 minutes before key events.

The Teacher's Energy Audit

Purpose: Build sustainable self-care routines.

Implementation Steps:
1. Set a timer for 10 minutes.
2. List all your weekly tasks and label each as energizing, neutral, or draining.
3. Add or schedule one energizing task each day (e.g., a walk, music).

4. Identify one draining activity to reduce or delegate.

Success Metrics:
Your energy levels even out over the week, and you recover from setbacks more quickly (Flook et al., 2013).

Adaptation:
If pressed for time, do a mini-audit midweek. Enlist a peer for accountability.

Integration:
Review your list during Sunday planning.

Mindful Lesson Planning Method

Purpose: Ease lesson preparation stress while enhancing classroom focus.

Implementation Steps:

1. Spend two minutes before planning to check in with your breath.
2. Set a realistic intention for the lesson (e.g., "Students will learn one new concept").
3. When distracted, gently return your focus to your intention.
4. After planning, list one thing you're looking forward to teaching.

Success Metrics:
You notice less mental fatigue and smoother classroom performance; students respond more positively to lessons (Tarissa Hidajat et al., 2023).

Adaptation:
Use 60-second breath checks in hectic weeks.

Integration:
Bookmark mindfulness reminders on your planning documents.

For international teachers adapting to unfamiliar evaluation systems, or recent graduates facing first observations, regular use of these concrete tools turns stress and critique into classroom confidence and long-term effectiveness. These exercises weave together the essential skills of feedback management and self-care, equipping new educators to navigate certification with clarity and resilience (Flook et al., 2013; Tarissa Hidajat et al., 2023).

Bringing It All Together

Now that we've explored the deep motivations behind teaching and the mindset skills needed for success, you're better prepared to face the path to certification with confidence. Remember, your commitment goes beyond passing exams — it's about making a real difference in students' lives and growing through every challenge. By embracing self-reflection, setting clear goals, seeking support, and managing feedback and stress mindfully, you can navigate doubts and setbacks as part of your journey. Keep focusing on progress, not perfection, and know that each small step forward builds the strong, resilient educator you're becoming. The road may have bumps, but your purpose, and persistence will carry you toward a rewarding and impactful teaching career.

Your why is the starting point for teaching however you must now learn how to teach. No one ever enters a profession and not learns the how of what they do. This is applicable to the field of education as well. One term that will be forever impressed on you educational thoughts is pedagogy. In our next chapter we will delve into the "how" of teaching.

Chapter 3:
Foundations First: Understanding Pedagogy

> "Those who know, do. Those who understand, teach."
> – Aristotle

As a school leader in this everchanging field we have had to be creative in the filling of teacher vacancies. According to the Learning Policy Institute as of June 2025 48 states including the District of Columbia employed an estimated 365,967 teachers who were not fully certified (Institute, 2025). Many of the teachers that I have hired had a strong knowledge of the content but struggled with how to teach it. I must admit that I had a teacher who was degreed in science and knew the ends and outs of all things science however he could not get the information to the students in a way that they learned the content. He did not know or understand the pedagogy of teaching. Pedagogy can be defined as the art and science of teaching. As you continue on your certification journey you must learn and understand how to teach.

Foundational Educational Theories and Applied Pedagogical Skills

Most people think teaching is all about having the right answers and standing in front of a classroom delivering facts. But the reality is quite different. Teaching is less about pouring knowledge into students' heads and more about guiding them to discover, question, and connect ideas on their own. It's also about understanding how each student thinks and learns, which means that one approach won't work for everyone. Behind every teacher's daily routine lies a web of theories and strategies that shape how lessons are planned, how students are supported, and how classrooms become places where everyone can thrive. Whether you're stepping into teaching for the first time, switching careers, preparing to take certification exams, or navigating a new education system, knowing these foundational ideas changes everything about how you approach your role and impact your students.

Foundations of Educational Theory

Constructivism puts students at the center of the learning process. In this approach, students are seen as active participants who build new knowledge by connecting it to what they already know. Rather than just absorbing information from a textbook or a lecture, learners explore, ask questions, and experiment. Student-centered learning values curiosity and encourages students to discover answers on their own, with the teacher playing the role of a guide or facilitator instead of simply delivering facts (McLeod, 2025). For example, imagine a science classroom where students investigate why plants grow toward the light. Instead of being told the answer, they make predictions, observe plants under different conditions, share findings, and refine their understanding with teacher support.

This active classroom environment fosters deeper understanding. Teachers help students make sense of new concepts by connecting them to students' personal experiences and prior knowledge. If a class discusses historical events, the teacher might start by asking students what they already know or how they feel about a current event. These connections help students create mental links, making learning more meaningful and memorable. Constructivist classrooms also use strategies such as hands-on experiments, collaborative projects, think-pair-share discussions, and creative problem-solving tasks. Instead of memorizing formulas, students work through real-world problems, reflect on their process, and collaborate with classmates.

Learning becomes more than an individual effort — social interaction is key. When students explain their reasoning, challenge ideas, and work in diverse groups, they strengthen their understanding (McLeod, 2025).

Teachers in constructivist classrooms take on important roles beyond simply delivering content. They assess students' knowledge by listening and observing, provide just enough hints or support to move learners forward, and gradually step back as students gain confidence. This method of providing support while encouraging independence is called scaffolding. For instance, before a group research project, a teacher might model how to find reliable sources, then offer guidance and feedback without giving away answers. As students gain skills, the teacher reduces support, fostering self-reliance and problem-solving ability (McLeod, 2025).

Behaviorism, in contrast, centers on how behavior is shaped by responses to the environment. This theory views learning as a process of acquiring new behaviors through reinforcement by being either positive or negative. Positive reinforcement rewards desirable actions, motivating students to repeat them. For example, a teacher might give verbal praise, stickers, or extra free time to students who complete their assignments on time. Negative reinforcement involves removing something unpleasant when a student behaves as desired, such as allowing students to skip a difficult task after showing consistent effort (National University, 2022).

In practice, behaviorist strategies support effective classroom management. Teachers set clear expectations and consistently apply rules and consequences. This predictability helps students feel secure and understand what is expected. If a student talks out of turn, a warning might be followed by a loss of privileges only if the behavior continues. On the flip side, positive recognition for staying on task reinforces good habits. Tools like behavior charts, reward systems, and timed routines help students monitor their progress and stay motivated (National University, 2022).

Behavior modification techniques rooted in behaviorism can address persistent challenges. For students struggling with completing homework, a teacher may set up a chart tracking assignments and reward completion with special activities. For disruptive behavior, the teacher might use time-outs or require apologies while also offering opportunities for students to earn back privileges. The key is consistency: students thrive when teachers reliably reinforce expectations and follow through on consequences.

Daily teaching practices often blend these approaches. Constructivism invites teachers to stay curious about their students' thinking, while behaviorism provides tools to shape a productive, safe classroom climate. Both theories help new teachers anticipate challenges. For instance, constructivist strategies require flexibility; students may uncover misconceptions or take time to reach correct answers, and teachers need patience to guide the process. With behaviorism, it's easy to rely too heavily on rewards or punishments and risk overlooking students' intrinsic motivation. Finding a balance between sparking curiosity and enjoyment while providing structure and clear consequences creates the best environment for learning (National University, 2022; McLeod, 2025).

As students actively participate, ask questions, make mistakes, and receive feedback, their cognitive development is supported. Students' learning styles, or the different ways they approach understanding new information, are also respected through a mix of discussion, hands-on activities, visuals, and written tasks. These foundational theories lay the groundwork for more advanced ideas about how children's minds develop and how social contexts influence learning, setting the stage for exploring the contributions of Piaget and Vygotsky.

Cognitive and Cultural Approaches in the Classroom

Understanding how children grow as thinkers and learners is essential for every teacher. Piaget's theory of cognitive development is a roadmap for tracking this growth as it unfolds in four main stages. Each stage comes with its own set of behaviors and learning strengths. When teachers recognize what stage a student is in, they can choose tasks and supports that match students' developmental readiness, making lessons much more effective (McLeod, 2025; (PDF) Piagetian and Vygotskian Approaches to Cognitive Development in the Kindergarten Classroom, n.d.).

Piaget's Stages of Cognitive Development

Children start in the sensorimotor stage, from birth to about two years old. Here, learning comes through direct physical interaction of reaching, grabbing, and tasting. In infancy, students respond best to rich sensory activities like touching different fabrics, playing with blocks, or watching bubbles float. Teachers can support this stage by providing plenty of safe objects to explore and talk about ("This is soft, this is bumpy"), and by pointing out new things together.

Between two and seven years old, children enter the preoperational stage. Their thinking is more imaginative and symbolic, but still quite limited. For example, a five-year-old might use a stick as a "magic wand" during pretend play but have trouble seeing things from another person's perspective. In class, a child may insist that there is more water in a tall, skinny glass than in a short, wide one, not realizing both actually hold the same amount. Teachers can use props, dramatic play, and simple models to help bridge the gap between imagination and reality.

Asking students to explain their thinking ("Why do you think the glass with more water is bigger?") helps them practice reasoning.

The concrete operational stage, ages seven to eleven, is when logical thinking starts to take shape, but still relies on concrete experiences. Students can now perform tasks that involve conservation, classification, and seriation. For instance, an eight-year-old can understand that a handful of clay is the same amount no matter how it's shaped. At this stage, children benefit from experiments and problem-solving tasks that let them manipulate real objects like measuring water, sorting objects, or planning group projects.

By age eleven and up, students reach the formal operational stage, where abstract reasoning becomes possible. They can imagine "what if" scenarios and solve problems without having everything right in front of them. Middle schoolers start to think more about ethics, fairness, and hypothetical situations. Teachers can encourage this stage by using open-ended questions, debates, and encouraging students to consider different viewpoints or design scientific investigations (McLeod, 2025).

To pinpoint a child's stage, teachers observe how the child solves problems, explains choices, and uses language. For example, if a second grader still chooses a tall beaker as "having more" despite being shown the quantities are equal, this points to preoperational thinking. Teachers stay alert to language use, logical consistency, and the ability to work with abstract ideas.

Vygotsky's Zone of Proximal Development and Scaffolding

While Piaget focused on fixed stages, Vygotsky highlighted the critical role of social interaction, language, and guidance. His idea of the "zone of proximal development" (ZPD) refers to the range between what a child can do alone and what they can achieve with support. Teachers use scaffolding and temporary supports like hints, modeling, or asking guiding questions to help students stretch beyond their current skill level. For example, when a group works together to write a story, a teacher might model a paragraph, then let students write their own while offering feedback. Peers can also act as tutors, explaining steps and offering encouragement ((PDF) Piagetian and Vygotskian Approaches to Cognitive Development in the Kindergarten Classroom, n.d.).

Culturally Responsive Teaching

Effective teaching honors every learner's cultural identity and background. Culturally responsive teaching means weaving students' cultures, languages, and traditions into lessons and classroom routines. This starts with getting to know families and students' home experiences, incorporating books and materials that reflect a range of backgrounds, and inviting students to share stories from their own cultures.

Teachers can revise traditional lessons by allowing students to solve math problems using examples from their community or by reading aloud from multicultural literature. Group projects can be organized to celebrate different holidays or foods represented in the classroom. Making space for multiple perspectives helps all children see themselves in the curriculum and value diversity in others ((PDF) Piagetian and Vygotskian Approaches to Cognitive Development in the Kindergarten Classroom, n.d.).

Inclusive classrooms also involve rethinking discipline and expectations. Teachers work to recognize cultural norms around talking, collaborating, and expressing opinions. Instead of a one-size-fits-all approach, teachers offer flexible seating, encourage bilingual communication, and adapt assignments so every student can participate meaningfully.

Such strategies do more than create a welcoming climate they boost engagement and achievement. Students who feel seen and respected are more likely to participate, take risks, and persist through challenges. When instruction is both developmentally and culturally responsive, every child is supported to reach their highest potential (McLeod, 2025; (PDF) Piagetian and Vygotskian Approaches to Cognitive Development in the Kindergarten Classroom, n.d.).

So now that we have gone over the educational theories let's connect theory to pedagogy. Pedagogy is a term that you will hear and use throughout your certification journey. In simple terms pedagogy is how a teacher teaches. Add this term to your mental dictionary.

Applying Theory Through Pedagogical Skills

Teachers turn educational theory into everyday classroom routines by weaving ideas about cognitive development and culturally responsive teaching into lesson design. When structuring a new unit, effective teachers write learning objectives that reflect what their students need to know and be able to do. For example, if a lesson aims for students to compare conflicting viewpoints on a historical event, the objective might be: "Students will be able to analyze and compare multiple perspectives." This aligns with higher-order cognitive skills by encouraging students to use critical thinking rather than just memorize facts. The teacher then picks activities that directly support these objectives, such as structured debates or comparison charts, and ensures materials reflect students' backgrounds and experiences for increased engagement and inclusivity (Carnegie Mellon University, 2019).

Making sure assessments match lesson goals is crucial for solid classroom practice. Teachers use formative assessments constantly to check in on student learning while instruction is happening. These might include short online quizzes, journal entries responding to a prompt, or a quick class discussion where students share what they've learned so far. A teacher could ask students to write a paragraph on what they think is the theme of a story, collect these, and provide specific feedback tied to the rubric. Students can then revise their work before final submission, which not only boosts understanding but also builds confidence as they see their progress (Poorvu Center for Teaching and Learning, 2021). Peer feedback activities work well at this stage, too, because they let students see other perspectives and practice self-reflection.

Summative assessments, on the other hand, are planned at the end of a unit or term. Examples might include major projects, cumulative exams, or presentations. Teachers make the expectations clear by sharing rubrics ahead of time, which helps students understand how their work will be judged and feel more in control of the outcome. If students will be designing a website or writing a research paper, the rubric would outline which elements count most and how points are assigned, tying back to the lesson's main objectives (Poorvu Center for Teaching and Learning, 2021). Blind grading is another practical option that helps keep grading fair and unbiased. Both formative and summative data become tools for teachers, informing which lessons might need to be retaught or which students need extra support.

Differentiation is about making sure every student finds a way into the learning, no matter their level or background. Teachers can start by offering assignments at different levels of complexity, such as giving reading passages at various levels of text difficulty while still covering the essential content. A reading group might work with more challenging primary sources, while another group reads a simpler summary and discusses it. This keeps all students on the same topic while respecting their readiness (Carnegie Mellon University, 2019). Teachers can also differentiate by product, allowing choice in how students demonstrate understanding — a written report, a recorded explanation, or even a skit.

Grouping strategies also support differentiation. Sometimes, strategic pairing works: a stronger reader teams up with a peer to tackle a difficult task together. Other times, interest-based groupings let students connect with material in a way that feels meaningful to them.

Assignments can be modified, too. For example, a math task might be adjusted for some students by offering guiding questions or visual cues, while advanced learners receive a challenge problem requiring deeper analysis. The learning objective doesn't change, but the path to reaching it is adjusted for each learner.

Self-reflection is the thread that ties classroom practice together. Teachers practice reflection by checking their own notes after a lesson, jotting down what worked well and what didn't.

Reviewing student responses from an exit ticket which is a quick, anonymous slip where students share what they learned that day can offer immediate insights into which concepts landed and which need reteaching (Poorvu Center for Teaching and Learning, 2021). Looking at assessment data over time, such as growth on writing assignments or performance on unit tests, helps teachers spot patterns and adjust instruction. For example, if several students missed a key science concept on an end of unit test, the teacher might decide to reteach the idea using a new hands-on activity. Sharing these findings with colleagues in team meetings or inviting feedback from students further informs and strengthens teaching practice. Through this regular cycle of reflection, adjustment, and growth, theoretical knowledge comes to life in the classroom, making learning meaningful and accessible for all students.

Bringing It All Together

Now that you've explored the key educational theories and practical teaching strategies that form the foundation of effective classroom practice, you're better equipped to step confidently into the world of teaching. Understanding how students think, learn, and interact helps you create lessons that engage and support every learner, while blending theory with hands-on approaches ensures your teaching is both meaningful and adaptable. Whether you're just starting out, changing careers, or preparing for certification exams, these tools will guide you in building a positive, inclusive classroom where all students can thrive. With this groundwork laid, you're ready to dive deeper into the exciting journey of becoming a skilled, responsive, and inspiring teacher and become familiar with the requirements for becoming a certified teacher.

Chapter 4:
Certification Requirements Demystified

"Better than a thousand days of diligent study is one day with a great teacher." Japanese proverb

Mastering Teacher Certification: Understanding Academic and Exam Requirements

"When I first started thinking about becoming a teacher, I felt completely lost," Maria said one afternoon during a casual chat with a friend. "I had no idea what classes I needed, whether my old college credits would count, or how to even sign up for the certification exams. It all seemed so confusing and overwhelming." Like many others stepping into this path, from recent grads to those switching careers ,Maria's story is not unusual. The process of getting certified can feel like a maze filled with complex rules, different degree options, tricky credit transfers, and demanding tests. People often find themselves asking: What courses should I take? How long will it really take? And most importantly, how do I prepare without wasting time or money? This chapter takes a close look at these questions, breaking down the academic hoops and exam hurdles that stand between aspiring teachers and their new careers. Through understanding the details of degrees, credits, specializations, and testing, readers can begin to see a clearer way forward even if they start out feeling as uncertain as Maria once did.

Academic Foundations and Program Choices

Minimum degree requirements for teacher certification are set by each state. In most cases, a bachelor's degree is the starting point. For general classroom teaching, a Bachelor of Arts (BA) or Bachelor of Science (BS) in education is the preferred degree. Some states, like New York, require a bachelor's degree that includes both a strong general education core and coursework in a content area or specialty subject. Candidates interested in areas like music, art, physical education, or technology education must complete degree programs aligned with those subjects, sometimes with additional credit requirements. For example, a candidate hoping to teach high school chemistry needs a degree with substantial coursework in chemistry. If someone seeks certification to teach a special subject like dance or family and consumer sciences, New York requires at least 30 semester hours which is a full major, in the specific content area, except for computer science and indigenous studies, which have different minimums (12 and 18 semester hours respectively) (*General and Program Specific Requirements for Teaching a Special Subject for Teacher Certification*, 2024).

Teaching programs come in two main forms: undergraduate and post-baccalaureate. The undergraduate path is common for recent high school graduates. Students enroll in combined programs where they earn a bachelor's degree and complete teacher preparation courses together. This typically involves four years of full-time study, not including student teaching. Common courses include "Educational Psychology," "Literacy Development," and "Methods of Teaching." The advantage here is efficiency. Both the degree and the certification coursework are completed together, often with built-in classroom experience. The challenge is the up-front time commitment, as students must plan early and dedicate at least four years to education study before entering the workforce.

The post-baccalaureate option is for those who already have a bachelor's degree, often in a field outside of education. These candidates enroll in certification-only programs or master's degree plus certification programs. Certification-only tracks can be completed in as little as one year full time if prerequisites have been met. Master's programs ("Master of Arts in Teaching," for example) usually take one to three years depending on part-time or full-time enrollment and prior coursework (TEACH, 2010). These routes are popular for career changers and those who discovered an interest in teaching later. The advantages include focused teacher training for mature students, but there can be higher tuition costs and less opportunity for undergraduate financial aid. Certification-only programs are typically less expensive and faster, but lack the advanced degree advantage that comes with a master's. On the other hand, a master's program can lead to a higher starting salary and is often required for advancement to a professional teaching certificate. Many successful post-bac candidates are motivated, have clear goals, and are prepared for intense, fast-paced coursework.

Specialization choices shape both academic planning and future career paths. Candidates select a subject and often a grade range. Subjects vary, but common choices include early childhood education, elementary education, English, mathematics, science, social studies, and visual or performing arts. Each specialization has specific requirements. For instance, in New York, most special subject certifications need 30 semester hours in the content core, but computer science requires only 12 semester hours, and indigenous culture/language studies need 18 semester hours (General and Program Specific Requirements for Teaching a Special Subject for Teacher Certification, 2024). Candidates can seek additional endorsements or combine areas — such as earning certification in both English and special education, or elementary and bilingual education. These combinations often expand employment prospects, especially in high-need areas or districts serving multilingual communities. Such dual endorsements require candidates to complete a full major (or its equivalent) in their first subject, with 18 credit hours required for each additional area of certification.

Grade-level certifications help further define a teacher's focus. Options generally include early childhood (pre-K–2), childhood (grades 1–6), middle childhood (grades 5–9), and adolescence (grades 7–12). Teacher candidates often take courses like "Literacy Methods for Early Learners," "Child Development," or "Classroom Management for Adolescent Learners" to meet these

grade-specific requirements. Fieldwork placements or student teaching are matched to the intended grade band, giving candidates hands-on experience with the appropriate age group.

Examination of coursework and credit requirements shows that all pathways must satisfy basic curriculum guidelines: general education, content core, and pedagogical core. Pedagogical core coursework covers child development, classroom management, students with disabilities, and language acquisition (General and Program Specific Requirements for Teaching a Special Subject for Teacher Certification, 2024). Three semester hours are dedicated to understanding students with disabilities, with additional coursework in formal assessment and instructional technology. Credit from previous degrees may transfer, especially for content core classes, reducing time and cost for candidates who already hold relevant coursework. This flexibility is vital for career changers, who frequently ask if their science, arts, or language classes will count toward certification prerequisites (TEACH, 2010).

Choosing the right degree and program leads directly to meeting these coursework and credit rules. Candidates who understand their options and select a clear specialization can create a smoother path through prerequisite courses, transfer credits, and student teaching placements, resulting in timely certification and employment.

Coursework Requirements and Credit Management; Core Coursework for Teacher Certification

To begin a career in teaching, aspiring educators must complete a defined sequence of core courses, regardless of whether they enter the field through traditional or alternative certification pathways. Educational psychology is foundational, providing insights into how students learn and develop. This coursework explores theories of motivation, classroom management, and child and adolescent development. Teaching methods or pedagogy classes focus on instructional strategies, lesson planning, and assessment creation. These courses build the practical skills required for day-to-day teaching. Subject-specific content courses ensure candidates are knowledgeable in the subjects they plan to teach, such as mathematics, English, science, or social studies. For example, a candidate preparing to teach biology must complete coursework in fundamental and advanced biology topics.

Field experiences, such as observation hours and supervised student teaching, are also standard requirements. Most programs require one or two semesters of student teaching during the last year, with candidates taking on increasing classroom responsibilities under the supervision of a mentor teacher. In some certification routes, fieldwork is paired with ongoing coursework, allowing students to immediately apply pedagogical skills in real classrooms (Strange, 2014).

Some institutions, like Texas Tech University, incorporate immersive field experiences as part of degree completion, ensuring hands-on readiness for the workforce (Degree Requirements | Advising | College of Education | TTU, 2025).

Transfer Credit Strategies

For aspiring teachers transferring from other colleges or switching careers, maximizing transfer credits saves both time and money. The first step is evaluating course equivalency. Candidates should gather detailed descriptions or syllabi of completed courses and compare them to the requirements of their intended program. Most colleges publish an official transfer guide or database listing which external courses have been previously accepted as equivalent. When in doubt, students can request a formal evaluation through the teacher education office or registrar.

Proper documentation is essential. Providing transcripts, course outlines, and official descriptions expedites the process and gives the receiving institution enough information to verify content alignment. Occasionally, syllabi from several years back or from less commonly recognized institutions may require further review by faculty committees to determine equivalency.

There are also common transfer restrictions to consider. Upper-division (junior and senior level) coursework is typically harder to transfer than introductory courses. Some programs require that a minimum number of credits be earned at the granting institution, especially within the final two years. For example, Texas Tech University mandates 42 hours of upper-division courses and sets requirements for communications literacy and multicultural coursework, which might not be met by lower-division credits received elsewhere (Degree Requirements | Advising | College of Education | TTU, 2025).

A real-world example involves a transfer student moving from a community college after earning 60 credits. Successfully transferred general education credits, including math and English, allow the student to focus exclusively on advanced pedagogy, subject content courses, and required field experiences. However, a challenge is that some courses, like specialized methods classes or local curriculum seminars, may not find a direct equivalent and must be retaken. Documentation showing alignment with course objectives can sometimes sway an academic advisor to accept a transfer when guidelines are ambiguous.

Academic Planning Strategies

Creating an efficient academic plan begins with mapping out all required courses and prerequisites. Many institutions provide sample four-year plans or templates, which list courses semester by semester. For career changers, alternative program coordinators might offer "fast-track" sequences that condense coursework into intensive summer terms and evening classes, making it possible to fulfill requirements while working.

Identifying and addressing knowledge gaps early ensures timely progress. If a future science teacher discovers they lack coursework in physics, they can plan to take this requirement online or at a local college before major pedagogy semesters. Checking prerequisite chains is crucial, Some upper-level pedagogy courses require prior completion of foundational topics. Missing one class can delay graduation by a year if not caught early.

Coordination with academic advisors is key. Advisors can clarify degree audit reports, recommend summer or online courses to stay on track, and inform candidates about recent curriculum changes. In some cases, advisors can petition for substitution or credit-by-exam opportunities, especially for career changers with extensive job experience or prior graduate coursework.

Resources for academic support extend beyond advising. Many colleges run tutoring centers for difficult subject matter, writing labs for literacy courses, and mentorship programs pairing new students with seniors. Online platforms may offer planning tools that simulate various course sequences and visualize how each semester fits with certification timelines.

By staying proactive in tracking prerequisites, consulting advisors regularly, and leveraging support services, both traditional undergraduates and career changers can navigate degree complexities and ensure eligibility for certification assessments. Effective planning, whether pursuing a standard four-year education degree or an alternative certification program, enables candidates to move confidently through their academic pathway and reach their goal of entering the classroom as certified teachers (Strange, 2014; Degree Requirements | Advising | College of Education | TTU, 2025).

Certification Exams and Preparation

Aspiring educators in Texas must meet specific examination requirements after finishing their academic coursework. The state structures the certification process so that candidates prove their subject knowledge and instructional skills through a set of required exams, each backed by clearly defined rules and timelines (Agency, 2021; Agency, 2023). Understanding how these exams work, what they test, and how to prepare efficiently gives candidates a solid advantage as they move from coursework to the classroom.

Types of Certification Exams

The certification exams that are required vary from state to state. Some states use the Praxis exam for teacher certification. California, Florida, Michigan, Arizona, Illinois and Texas have their own certification exam. Refer to the Appendix to see in detail what is required for teacher certification by state.

Texas teacher certification exams fall into two main types: content area assessments and pedagogy assessments. The content exams, such as the Texas Examinations of Educator Standards (TExES), test a candidate's grasp of subject-specific knowledge. For example, a future math teacher will answer questions covering key algebraic concepts, probability, and calculus.

Similarly, someone seeking English Language Arts certification will interpret literature, analyze complex texts, and demonstrate their understanding of grammar and composition.

Pedagogy exams, including those covering the Pedagogy and Professional Responsibilities (PPR), focus on the art and science of teaching. These exams present scenarios involving classroom management, ethical dilemmas, lesson delivery, and data-driven instruction.

Candidates might be asked how to respond when a student consistently disrupts class or how to adapt lessons for students with varied learning needs.

Both exam types often combine multiple-choice and constructed-response formats, requiring candidates to think analytically and apply theory to practice. For instance, a pedagogy exam may ask for an essay outlining step-by-step approaches to differentiated instruction, or present a classroom dilemma and request a detailed action plan.

Key Exam Components

Certification exams share several common components designed to assess a range of educator competencies. The multiple-choice section typically accounts for 60–80% of the test, with most exams lasting around four hours. Candidates can expect 80 to 120 questions, each targeting key subject matter or teaching principles. Multiple-choice items might ask for the most effective assessment strategy for a given scenario or the next instructional steps after a formative assessment reveals gaps.

Constructed-response tasks, found in both content and pedagogy tests, require test-takers to provide written explanations or solutions. For example, a math content exam could ask for a detailed method to solve an equation, while a pedagogy test might request an analysis of classroom data to propose improvements. Time management is vital, since constructed-response sections may allow 30–45 minutes per prompt and are scored based on clarity, logic, and use of evidence.

Performance assessments, such as portfolios or recorded teaching sessions, sometimes supplement traditional exams. These tasks evaluate the ability to plan, deliver, and reflect on real lessons. A candidate might submit a video lesson and written analysis showing how they engaged students and adjusted instruction based on feedback.

Test Preparation Strategies

Effective test preparation balances deep content review with practical test-taking skills. Successful candidates often start by reviewing the state's official exam frameworks, which outline the topics and skills tested (Agency, 2023). Creating a study schedule that spans eight to ten weeks helps break down large subjects into smaller, daily tasks. Candidates usually dedicate the first phase to content mastery, such as using flashcards for key terms or teaching difficult concepts aloud to a peer. Midway through, they transition to applying knowledge through practice tests that mirror the real exam's format.

One powerful approach is to alternate between subject review and pedagogical case studies, ensuring both types of readiness develop in tandem. For instance, candidates might spend mornings reviewing lesson planning strategies and afternoons working through sample biology or history problems, followed by short quizzes. Participating in group study sessions or online forums also helps clarify confusing topics and introduces multiple perspectives to problem-solving.

Registration, Fees, and Logistics

Registration for Texas educator exams takes place online, with each assessment typically cost beginning at $116 with additional fees for various test codes (Agency, 2025). Exam windows are offered year-round, but registration deadlines fall about four to six weeks before the desired test date. Candidates should review the test vendor's calendar and secure a seat early, especially for high-demand times like summer or winter breaks.

For candidates needing financial support, educator preparation programs may offer exam voucher codes, reducing or waiving fees for eligible participants. Applicants typically demonstrate need based on income or participation in specific training programs. To apply, candidates complete online forms with supporting documentation.

If unexpected life events require a change, rescheduling is possible for a modest fee — usually around $35 if done at least 48 hours in advance. Candidates who do not pass a test may retake it, but some states limit the number of attempts a potential educator can take the exam. The state of Texas limits the attempts to five per exam. After reaching the cap, an official waiver application, including a statement of preparation and supporting evidence, is required to pursue additional tries (Agency, 2021).

Realistically, these steps require persistence and care. By approaching each component with a systematic plan and an eye on logistics, aspiring Texas educators can set themselves up for success on the journey to certification.

Other states take various test for teacher certification. In the Appendix is a list stating what test is required in each state:

Bringing It All Together

Now that we've broken down the key steps of teacher certification — from choosing the right degree and program, managing coursework and credits, to preparing for and passing your exams — you have a clear roadmap to guide your journey into teaching. Whether you're starting fresh, changing careers, or navigating the process from another country, understanding these essentials helps you plan with confidence and avoid unnecessary hurdles. With this knowledge in hand, you're better equipped to make informed decisions, stay on track academically, and approach certification exams with a focused strategy. The path may feel challenging at times, but each step brings you closer to joining the rewarding world of education where you can make a real difference.

An additional component on you journey to certification is the student teaching experience. We will delve into all that student teaching entails in the upcoming chapter.

Chapter 5:
Classroom Realities: The Student Teaching Experience

Making the Most of Your Student Teaching Practicum

I'll never forget the first morning of my student teaching placement. I sat in my car in the school parking lot gripping the steering wheel, my stomach in knots. I had spent weeks preparing lesson plans and imagining what this day would be like, but in that moment, all I could feel was fear. What if the students didn't respect me? What if I froze in the middle of a lesson? What if I simply wasn't cut out to be a teacher?

Walking into the classroom, my mentor teacher welcomed me warmly, but my nerves didn't settle. When she introduced me to the students, I could feel my heart racing as twenty pairs of eyes turned toward me. I smiled, but inside I was shaking. The first time I led a small group activity, my voice trembled and I clutched my papers so tightly my knuckles turned white. I was convinced they could see right through me — that they knew I was scared.

That fear followed me home every night. I replayed the day's events, second-guessing every word and decision. I even cried once, wondering if I was strong enough for this profession.

But slowly, things began to shift. My mentor reminded me that confidence comes with practice, and she celebrated my small successes. The students, too, surprised me — they were kinder and more forgiving than I expected. One day, a student raised her hand and said, "I like how you explain things." That small comment gave me the courage to try again the next day with a little more confidence.

By the end of the semester, I still felt nervous before teaching, but it wasn't the paralyzing fear I once carried. Instead, it became a reminder that I cared deeply about doing well. What began as fear grew into resilience, and I walked away from my student teaching experience knowing that while I might not have all the answers, I had the heart, patience, and persistence to become the teacher I always hoped to be. - This was the experience of a prospective teacher I supervised during their certification journey.

Did you know that completing a student teaching practicum is a required step for nearly all teacher certification programs in the United States? It's the moment when what you've learned in textbooks and lectures meets the real, everyday challenges of a classroom. If you're wondering how to navigate this hands-on experience successfully, or what it really takes to grow from a student into a confident teacher, you're not alone. Many new educators and career changers face these questions as they prepare to enter the classroom. This chapter will help you understand the role of your practicum and equip you with practical strategies to make the most of this key phase on your path to becoming a certified teacher.

Entering the Practicum: Core Responsibilities and Building Mentor Relationships

Student teaching is where theory from your college coursework meets the lively, sometimes unpredictable world of the classroom. Every aspiring teacher in a certification program is required to complete this hands-on phase before earning a teaching license. Think of student teaching as the bridge that helps you cross from knowing about teaching to becoming a capable, reflective teacher in your own right. During this time, you step into a real classroom, work alongside an experienced educator, and start to shape your professional identity, one lesson, one interaction at a time (Goldshaft,

2024).

Stepping into your mentor's classroom, you may notice right away that their role extends far beyond supervisor. Good mentors do more than observe from the back and fill out checklists. They invite you into co-planning lessons, sometimes asking you which activities you feel excited to try or which objectives you want to focus on. You might work together to map out the day's learning targets: perhaps deciding how to introduce multiplication strategies to fifth graders, or how to adapt a social studies discussion so every student feels heard.

Mentors also model classroom management, both by their own daily routines and by walking you through the details. For example, they might demonstrate how to get the class's attention using a simple hand signal or share strategies for helping a distracted student reconnect with the task. When you run your first small-group reading session, the mentor may sit nearby, jotting down notes. Afterward, they share praise for how warmly you greeted the students, but also point out if transitions between activities felt rushed. This specific, practical feedback is priceless, not just "Good job," but even specific feedback such as, "Try giving a two-minute warning before wrapping up; it helps students finish strong" (Goldshaft, 2024). These specifics are nuances that develop one into a seasoned educator.

At the start, your teaching responsibilities focus on bite-sized pieces rather than full control of the classroom. You might begin by helping to take attendance, passing out materials, or leading a warm-up activity. Some student teachers start with read-alouds at the carpet or guiding a simple math center. As you get comfortable, you take on bigger slices of the day — planning and teaching a whole lesson, possibly in your best subject at first. For example, you might design a science experiment demonstration, choosing materials, writing the guiding questions, and deciding how to group the students so everyone tries the activity.

Even in your first week, you will see that classroom management is a skill learned step by step. Your mentor may ask you to monitor students as they work independently or handle a transition between activities. You observe which cues signal that a child needs help or when small conflicts pop up. Gradually, you try out different tone of voice, posture, and presence to see what keeps students focused or calms the class after recess. Each tiny success builds your confidence, from turning chaos into quiet by giving clear directions, to checking in with a shy learner at their desk.

Student teaching shines as a space for professional growth, with feedback sessions from your mentor at the heart of this process. These are dedicated moments when the teacher shares direct, yet supportive feedback. They may comment on your questioning technique, noting that you gave every student a chance to speak but could deepen the discussion by asking follow-up questions. You reflect together on what worked and what could improve, sometimes reviewing short video clips of your teaching or going over student work samples to see how your lesson landed (Goldshaft, 2024).

Mentors use several methods to evaluate your performance, including observation checklists, rubrics, and informal notes from each lesson. They may set concrete goals each week, such as "increase the use of open-ended questions" or "incorporate student voice into your lesson closure." With time, you start to notice your own progress — like when you handle a tricky classroom disruption smoothly or when a previously quiet student participates in your discussion (Pattison-Meek, 2024).

A common growth milestone is planning and leading a multi-day lesson sequence, where you build on student ideas and adapt when things don't go as planned. You might design a reading project, notice some students lagging, and work with your mentor to adjust grouping strategies. Moments like these help you see that good teaching is about constantly noticing, reflecting, and making small changes that support every learner (Goldshaft, 2024).

Welcoming advice from students can also enhance your practicum.

Some mentors encourage student teachers to ask learners what helps them focus or what makes lessons more engaging. One teacher-in-training might hold a quick feedback circle after a lesson: "What did you enjoy? What could be different?" (Pattison-Meek, 2024). Insights from students — like "I like when we work in teams" or "The instructions were hard to follow" — give you practical ideas to try in your next lesson.

Practicing reflection and seeking these varied sources of feedback set the tone for your ongoing professional journey. Each lesson, each tip, each adjustment helps you move closer to becoming an adaptable, thoughtful teacher — one who learns both from mentors and from students, always aiming to meet diverse learning needs (Goldshaft, 2024; Pattison-Meek, 2024).

Everyday Practice: Effective Strategies for Classroom Growth and Professional Standards

Creating a strong classroom presence starts with hands-on strategies that shape daily routines. Each morning, organizing materials, writing clear agendas on the board, and greeting students at the door help students ease into the day and set expectations. Teachers who post daily learning objectives signal a professional and purposeful environment. Keeping materials, handouts, and resources in labeled bins or folders reduces time lost to searching and helps students find what they need independently. Routines like turning in assignments to a specific tray, rotating classroom roles, and using checklists for clean-up foster self-reliance, allowing the class to flow smoothly from one activity to the next.

Taking the initiative to adapt lessons in real time demonstrates leadership. For example, when an activity seems to lag, adjusting instructions, adding movement, or switching to a group format boosts engagement. If students grasp a concept quickly, challenge them with an extension task or deeper question. Curating visuals, organizing digital content, or sourcing a hands-on prop for the next day highlights genuine investment in student learning. These habits show that student teachers see themselves as active facilitators rather than passive deliverers of set plans (iamalcorndev, 2022).

Feedback from mentor teachers is most effective when teachers treat observations as learning opportunities instead of critiques. After each teaching session, jotting down key points from the mentor's comments, such as reminders to circulate the room or suggestions about phrasing questions, helps solidify goals. Teachers who ask clarifying questions — "Could you share an example of how you model patience when a student gives a wrong answer?" — extract more actionable insights. Self-reflection deepens this process. At the end of each day, writing a brief reflection about what went well and what could have improved, such as classroom transitions or tone of voice, turns theory into practice. One student teacher, for example, noticed students were distracted during math centers. After re-reading mentor notes and reflecting, she restructured center rotations and used a visual timer the next day, resulting in smoother transitions and fewer disruptions.

Maintaining professional standards means teachers model ethical decision-making and foster trust daily. Treating each student's academic records and personal information with strict confidentiality — discussing learning disabilities or home situations only with administrative staff — ensures privacy is respected (iamalcorndev, 2022). Teachers use neutral language when describing students, avoid favoritism, and refrain from criticizing school policies in front of students.

Demonstrating punctuality, dressing appropriately, and communicating courteously with parents shows students and colleagues what professionalism means in action. When conflicts arise, teachers keep their cool, mediate fairly, and use school-approved channels to address issues. A student teacher who overhears hallway teasing, for instance, intervenes promptly yet discreetly, documenting the event and informing relevant staff.

Clear, consistent communication underpins classroom presence. Speaking at an audible, steady pace and pausing to invite questions make directions accessible to everyone. Teachers use gestures to emphasize key points, pointing to anchor charts, spreading arms to signal group work, or giving a reassuring thumbs-up for encouragement. Eye contact creates connection, while an open stance signals approachability. Building rapport involves daily routines like morning check-ins, remembering students' interests, and celebrating small wins. Calling on every student, not just the eager ones, and responding thoughtfully to their answers, fosters an inclusive environment.

During formal teacher observations, student teachers make the most of learning opportunities by using structured note-taking methods. They organize notes into columns: one for strategies used, another for student reactions, and a third for follow-up questions or ideas. By focusing attention on how a teacher manages transitions or regains focus after disruptions, observers collect specific, reproducible techniques. Afterward, analyzing which practices made lessons effective helps clarify what works best for certain age groups or content areas. For instance, if a mentor uses humor to redirect off-task behavior, a student teacher might experiment with light, positive comments tailored to their own personality. Reflecting on these observations in a journal and intentionally trying out new approaches the following week supports continuous growth.

Each of these habits contributes to a confident classroom presence and professional development. Consistent daily routines provide security, while openness to feedback and reflection fuels improvement. Ethical choices protect student dignity and foster a supportive classroom community. Clear communication and mindful body language invite engagement and trust. Close observation of mentor teachers, with attention to detail and analysis, helps aspiring educators blend best practices with their unique teaching styles, leading to a more effective and rewarding student teaching experience (iamalcorndev, 2022).

Maximizing the Practicum: Engagement, Documentation, and Preparation for Certification

Taking charge of your student teaching experience makes a lasting difference in your growth as an educator. Making the most of this practicum begins with stepping into each day with intention, treating every moment as an opportunity to stretch your skills and deepen your insight.

Proactive Engagement

Initiative sets you apart during a practicum. Arrive early to help set up the classroom or stay a bit later to assist with end-of-day organization. Offer to lead small-group instruction or support after-school activities, such as a reading club or a science fair committee, even if these tasks stretch your comfort zone. Volunteering to coordinate a classroom display or organize materials for a unit signals your dedication and versatility.

Asking purposeful questions is another hallmark of effective engagement. Inquire about the reasoning behind your mentor's classroom management choices or how they differentiate lessons for varied learning needs. Seek to understand not just the "what," but the "why" behind instructional methods. For example, if a mentor uses formative assessment strategies like exit tickets, ask about how the data shapes tomorrow's lesson.

Embrace collaboration beyond your mentor teacher. Connect with the special education team to learn about accommodations, or join planning sessions with grade-level colleagues. One student teacher, Mara, noticed her placement school emphasized vocabulary development schoolwide; she organized a shared digital folder where teachers could contribute and access engaging word games, positioning herself as a valuable team member.

Documentation of Professional Growth

Tracking your progress with purpose increases your learning return from each lesson. Start with an organized teaching journal, divided into sections such as daily reflections, lesson plans, observed strategies, and "aha moments." A typical entry might note how a lesson succeeded or why students struggled with a particular concept. Document questions that emerge during the day to revisit later with your mentor or through professional reading.

Artifacts capture the evidence of your journey. Collect copies of lesson plans, samples of student work (with names removed), observation feedback, photos of classroom displays you created, and communication logs with families (while observing school privacy policies). Keep a log of professional development sessions you attend, noting new techniques you intend to try.

Organize these artifacts in a digital folder or a binder with clear tabs for easy reference. Reviewing your documentation weekly uncovers patterns: perhaps your questioning strategies are improving, or you notice that lessons heavy on group work spark more engagement. This habit turns evidence collection into a powerful learning tool.

Evidence Collection

Showcasing your competency demands careful selection of evidence. Save copies of annotated lesson plans where you responded to prior feedback. Student learning outcomes serve as strong evidence; for instance, keep pre- and post-assessment results from a math mini-unit you taught. Charts of student progress or growth, graphs, and anecdotal records from reading conferences demonstrate your impact on learning.

Collect materials that highlight your professional development, such as notes from staff workshops or a summary of an online course you completed. A student teacher named Jordan created a portfolio section called "Growth in Action," where he included email exchanges with his mentor about lesson revisions, alongside screenshots of his revised work.

Presenting evidence clearly matters. Use captions to briefly explain the purpose of each item when assembling your teaching portfolio. For example, "This exit ticket analysis led me to reteach fractions using manipulatives." This helps mentors and hiring panels quickly see your thinking, responsiveness, and growth.

Practical Tips for Evidence Organization

- Use cloud storage services with folders by week or theme for easy retrieval
- Label files with dates and brief descriptions
- Set aside time weekly to curate and reflect on gathered evidence

Feedback Implementation

Consistently acting on feedback accelerates your professional growth. Develop a simple feedback log — this could be a spreadsheet or a notebook — where you record feedback after each observed lesson. Summarize the main points, note specific suggestions ("More wait time after asking questions"), and your own ideas for addressing them.

Review your log frequently and select one or two goals to address each week. Plan concrete actions, such as scripting open-ended questions before your next lesson or practicing transitions to reduce downtime. Try implementing changes, then seek targeted feedback to measure progress. For example, after a mentor suggests incorporating student-driven discussions, design and facilitate a literature circle, then invite your mentor to observe and discuss what went well and where you can push further.

Successful student teachers transform constructive criticism into steady, visible improvement. By actively documenting and reviewing the impact of these adjustments — perhaps through student engagement data or feedback from multiple observers — you demonstrate resilience and a commitment to evolving as an educator.

Concluding Thoughts

Now that you understand the many layers of the student teaching practicum — from building strong mentor relationships and mastering everyday classroom routines to actively engaging in your growth and carefully documenting your progress — you're well equipped to step confidently into this vital phase of your teaching journey. Embracing each challenge and feedback moment as a chance to learn will help you grow from theory into a skilled, thoughtful educator ready to meet diverse student needs. With intention, reflection, and a willingness to adapt, you can make the most of your practicum experience and take meaningful steps toward becoming a teacher who not only survives but thrives in the classroom and beyond.

Chapter 6:

State-by-State: Navigating Legal and Geographic Hurdles

Certification Application Process

Maria stared at the long list of documents and steps ahead of her, feeling overwhelmed. She had already passed her exams and finished her preparation program, but now the real challenge was beginning — the maze of forms, transcripts, background checks, and online portals. Each time she thought she had everything ready, she found out something was missing or needed correction. The process felt confusing and slow, and Maria wondered if there was a clear way to keep it all organized and move forward without constant setbacks. Many aspiring teachers like her face this exact struggle when trying to turn their hard work into an official certification that opens the door to the classroom.

Teacher certification is a state-managed process, meaning each state has its own pathways, requirements, and systems for credentialing educators. Understanding these distinctions is vital for prospective teachers, especially those who plan to relocate or seek reciprocal licensing across states. This chapter provides direct commentary on teacher certification systems across the U.S., highlighting best practices, common pitfalls, and standout features of select states. We will begin with emphasis on Texas and then delve into seeking certification in other states.

Navigating State Certification

Getting your state teaching certification might seem like a straightforward step after graduation, but it often turns into a maze of unexpected rules, tests, and deadlines. Each state has its own way of doing things, from different exams to unique paperwork requirements — and what works in one place might not work in another. This can make the path to becoming a licensed teacher feel more complicated than it should be.

This chapter breaks down those differences and shows you how to navigate the variety of certification processes across states. You'll learn why understanding each state's system matters, how to avoid common pitfalls, and practical ways to stay organized throughout the process. By the end, you'll be better equipped to take control of your certification journey — no matter where you plan to teach.

State Highlights and Teacher Reciprocity Overview

Teachers moving from college graduation to their first classroom find that certification is not a one-size-fits-all process. Requirements depend on the state and change things like test timelines, paperwork loads, and how many hoops you have to jump through if you're coming from somewhere else. One person's journey might take them through a few online forms and a quick background check. Someone else might need months of study, expensive tests, and long waits for transcripts to make their way through the bureaucracy.

California stands out for its paperwork, intricate test rules, and slow turnaround. The California Commission on Teacher Credentialing (CTC) is in charge. Applications run through an online portal also called CTC. Most candidates must pass the CBEST and CSET exams, which test general skills and subject knowledge. But the list of possible extra steps includes fingerprinting, training for English learners, and new requirements for reading instruction. Temporary credentials, like the "Intern Credential," allow some people to work while finishing requirements, but tracking all deadlines is critical. Out-of-state teachers will find that even with interstate agreements, the CTC often demands test comparisons and can deny waivers for exams like the RICA (Reading Instruction Competence Assessment), which adds months for some new arrivals.

New York uses layers: the Office of Teaching Initiatives (OTI) handles licensing through the TEACH online system. There are two common levels: the Initial Certificate, followed later by the Professional Certificate. Candidates take the Educating All Students (EAS) and Content Specialty Tests (CST), and — if you're headed for early childhood or special education — a Literacy exam. Even after you apply, getting the Initial Certificate can drag out, sometimes taking months if documentation is missing or if your education isn't a perfect match. Reciprocity here means new teachers from other states must often complete state workshops in Harassment, Child Abuse, and School Violence Prevention. Even those with years of classroom experience will find they need to jump through these training modules.

Florida has earned a reputation for being far more flexible. Managed by the Florida Department of Education through its online "Educator Certification Application System," the process works for both new and out-of-state candidates. The state's main hurdle is the Florida Teacher Certification Exam (FTCE). Still, if you hold a valid certificate from another state, Florida may grant a "Temporary Certificate" first, giving you up to three years to meet any missing requirements. This fast-track situation can help teachers land jobs while still finishing outstanding tests or coursework.

Arizona and Nevada both allow new teachers or out-of-state candidates to start with an "Intern" or "Provisional" Certificate. In Arizona, the State Board of Education provides a user-friendly application process online. Nevada uses the Nevada Department of Education's OPAL portal. In both states, candidates must complete Praxis exams but may teach while gathering missing coursework or tests. This makes these states forgiving for people who want to work right away, though they'll need to keep track of renewal rules.

Illinois presents a different sort of challenge. The Illinois State Board of Education handles credentials through the ELIS system. The pathway includes Test of Academic Proficiency (TAP) or ACT/SAT substitution, edTPA, and a content test. Out-of-state teachers must submit every transcript and test score, and reviews can take a long time. Illinois stands out for manual reviews of every application, which creates long processing times and can be frustrating for candidates on a tight hiring schedule.

Georgia, North Carolina, and Massachusetts each bring their own twist. Georgia uses the Georgia Professional Standards Commission's MyPSC portal. You'll take the GACE for your area. North Carolina requires the Praxis and a local reading test, with the ability for lateral-entry teachers to start in the classroom while finishing requirements. Massachusetts, run by the Department of Elementary and Secondary Education's ELAR portal, is known for the long MTEL test cycle and slow approvals, which can stretch for months. Out-of-state teachers often need to take state-specific tests, no matter their experience.

Reciprocity agreements draw new teachers to friendly states, but differences in testing requirements, background checks, and online systems create unexpected obstacles. Teachers who skip small application steps, forget documentation, or misjudge test timelines miss out on hiring windows or spend extra money fixing surprises. States may say they honor out-of-state credentials, but the actual experience rests on careful reading of rules and a solid checklist, so new teachers should always plan for more steps than they expect.

Avoiding Pitfalls and Effective Coaching Strategies

Mistakes and misconceptions surface almost everywhere new teachers undergo the state certification process. Each shared story about overlooked paperwork or misunderstood steps can point towards practical habits that help keep everything on track. Awareness by itself is a start, but shifting toward concrete tools and routines lets candidates move from uncertainty to control.

Understanding a state's certification portal forms the core of this approach. Every state education board tends to operate a unique online system for teacher applicants. The best first step is hands-on exploration. Once you know which state you plan to certify in, set aside time to create a user account — even if you're not applying immediately. Log in. Walk through each requirement. For instance, Texas calls their portal ECOS and links it to TEAL, while California applicants work through the CTC platform. They differ in layout, navigation, and even language. One person who taught in Illinois described feeling lost until she found the "Educator Licensure" page, months into her search. A friend in North Carolina tried searching for "teacher portal," only to learn their state called it "NC DPI Online Licensure System." By signing up early, you become familiar with where to find forms, track progress, and spot any unusual requirements.

A central piece of owning the certification process is developing a personal certification calendar. Backward planning works best here. Begin with the absolute last deadline for your application.

Instead of waiting until crunch time, chart every milestone you will need to clear. This list often includes:

- Exam registration and test dates
- Transcript request deadlines from your university
- Scheduling fingerprint background checks
- Gathering recommendation letters from your teaching

program or references
- Submission windows for key documents

By listing these out, you can assign each a specific date on your calendar, then add reminders a week or two beforehand. This keeps bottlenecks away. One past candidate who relied only on memory realized, the night before the paperwork deadline, she'd never ordered her official transcript. Adding digital calendar events and sticky-note reminders in her workspace helped her track future steps with less stress. A simple checklist or a spreadsheet, organized by each phase and requirement, can further prevent overlap or oversight.

Digital and physical document management deserves its own plan. For every state you apply to, make a separate folder in your computer and label it with the year. Do the same for a secure folder or envelope where you keep hard copies. Name each digital file with the state, your name, and the document type, like "NY_Jordan_Smith_BAtranscript_2024.pdf" so you avoid confusion later. Always request both an electronic and, if possible, a paper copy of transcripts and test scores, since many states still require originals or sealed versions. This habit pays off if the state's portal has technical issues; one applicant in Georgia had her digital file corrupted on the upload, but she had a copy and sent it right to the office. Never assume the testing agency or university will keep your documents on file forever. Download official score reports the day they are released and back them up to a cloud drive or external hard drive.

Building a "reciprocity toolkit" helps in case you ever apply out of state. At a minimum, store:

- Complete test score reports (with your name and test year visible)
- Several sealed, official transcripts
- Cleared fingerprint background checks
- Copies of recommendation letters, on official letterhead and signed

States sometimes clear out digital records. A former Alabama candidate learned, too late, that her test results were purged after two years. Because she didn't have a backup, she had to retake an exam she'd passed before. Collecting, downloading, and printing each requirement as soon as it's available saves plenty of time and worry.

Staying vigilant over document status in your state portal reduces waiting games. After you submit a test or course record, log in once a week to make sure the system shows it as "received" or "approved." Don't rely only on confirmation emails — sometimes those get lost or don't arrive at all. One Oregon graduate avoided a month-long delay by reviewing her submission portal two weeks ahead and noticing her scores had not posted. She called the testing agency and got it fixed in time.

Pay close attention to terminology. Each state uses its own words, and small misunderstandings can cause delays. Where one state's "intern" might mean a provisionally-certified teacher, another's might mean a classroom observer without standing. Reviewing definitions in your state's board of education documents clarifies each status. Several candidates have had applications stuck in review because they didn't realize "residency certificate" was different from a "provisional license." Researching this in advance avoids repeating application steps.

Approaching each step with an organizational, proactive mindset makes the process smoother. Candidates who set up every document before starting the application, who double-check portal entries and use calendar reminders, often don't face last-minute scrambles or repeated submissions. They feel more prepared and move on to teaching with confidence.

Now that you understand the twists and turns of state certification and reciprocity, you're better equipped to tackle the process without getting overwhelmed. By taking charge early — exploring your state's portal, setting clear deadlines, organizing your documents, and keeping a close eye on every step — you can avoid common pitfalls and move confidently toward your teaching career. Each state has its quirks, but with a solid plan and attention to detail, you'll turn what once seemed complicated into a manageable pathway that leads right to your first classroom.

Texas Certification Specifics: Compiling Required Documentation for Texas Teacher Certification

Getting started with the teacher certification process for Texas begins by gathering four types of documentation: official transcripts, test score documentation, background check materials, and program completion verification. This phase establishes the foundation for your certification application, so patience, organization, and diligence are key.

Official Transcripts

Requesting official transcripts from all colleges or universities attended is among the first tasks. Begin by logging into your former institution's registrar or records office website. Look for a "transcript request" or "education records" link, typically found in student services sections.

Some colleges use third-party services such as Parchment or the National Student Clearinghouse. When you place the order, select "official transcript" and ensure the degree conferral date appears on the document; omitting this step can cause delays or rejections later, as the Texas Education Agency (TEA) requires clear verification that your degree is conferred (Agency, 2023).

Electronic delivery is the fastest option, often taking 24-48 hours at a cost of $5-$15 per transcript. If your institution only mails documents and you are seeking Texas certification provide TEA's address — 1701 N. Congress Avenue, Austin, TX, 78701 — and allow 5-10 business days for processing and delivery (Agency, 2021). Before finalizing the order, double-check the recipient email, especially if sending transcripts electronically to educatecert@tea.texas.gov or the address a staff member gives you. If you are seeking certification in other states make sure you reach out to the various state education agencies for the state you are seeking certification. Refer to the list in the appendix. Always keep order confirmation emails as proof, and create a spreadsheet with dates, contact numbers, and tracking information for mailed documents. A common pitfall is sending unofficial copies or transcripts missing graduation dates, both of which can halt your application unexpectedly.

Test Score Documentation

Certification in Texas requires a series of standardized tests, such as the Texas Examinations of Educator Standards (TExES), the Pedagogy and Professional Responsibilities (PPR), and, for many candidates, the Science of Teaching Reading (STR) test. After completing your exam, log in to your Educator Certification Online System (ECOS) account accessed from secure.sbec.state.tx.us. If you registered with the wrong TEA ID, test scores may not link to your application. Always use your legal name exactly as it appears on your transcripts and TEA portal to avoid errors (Agency, 2023).

Score reporting is handled by Pearson, the exam administrator for Texas. In your Pearson account, verify that your most recent scores display as "Reported to TEA." Download and save PDFs of your score reports, keeping them in a digital folder labeled by test name and date. If you notice a missing score or "processing" status, contact Pearson customer support at (800)

877-4599 immediately, since delays can last weeks if left unaddressed. Costs for additional score reports sent to TEA typically range from $20-$30 per request. A screenshot of your Pearson dashboard, with a checkmark beside each required exam, can help reassure you that nothing is missed.

Background Check Materials

All teacher candidates must submit digital fingerprints through IdentoGO and undergo a criminal history background check. Start by registering on identogo.com using the TEA code provided during your application process. Enter personal information carefully, since mismatched details cause processing errors. After registration, select a convenient IdentoGO location — they're often found in UPS Stores or local offices in most Texas cities — and schedule your LiveScan fingerprint appointment.

Bring a valid, unexpired government ID such as a state driver's license or passport. Without appropriate identification, your appointment cannot proceed. At the appointment, a technician will scan your fingerprints electronically, a process that usually takes 10-15 minutes. Processing fees currently run about $50. Results are automatically transmitted to TEA within 3-7 business days, but can take longer during peak hiring seasons (Agency, 2021). Keep a copy of your IdentoGO appointment confirmation and check your ECOS dashboard for updates under "Background Check Status." A frequent mistake is scheduling under the wrong agency code, so always confirm your details on the registration summary screen before payment.

Program Completion Verification

If you're graduating from a Texas Educator Preparation Program (EPP), your final step is securing verification of your completion and recommendation for certification. Most EPPs initiate this automatically once you finish all coursework and field experiences. Confirm with your program advisor that you've met every requirement, including passing all necessary TExES and PPR exams. Request a copy of your completion certificate or recommendation email, as this serves as a formal record for your files.

EPPs submit required forms, such as the "Recommendation for Certification" and official program completion checklists, directly to TEA through internal portals. Verify your certification area — early childhood, elementary, secondary, or subject-specific — matches what appears in your TEA portal. Review your ECOS account to confirm the "EPP Recommendation" field is populated. If anything is missing or incorrect, notify your program immediately to avoid delays.

By following these detailed steps, tracking your progress, and maintaining open communication with certifying bodies, you'll build a robust and error-free certification document package — giving your Texas teacher certification journey a strong start (Agency, 2023; Agency, 2021).

Step-By-Step Instruction for Using the TEA Portal and Submitting Your Application

Before starting the online teacher certification application, you will need your transcripts, testing results, and background check materials ready. Gathering all your documentation beforehand makes the process much smoother and decreases the chance of errors or delays (2025). The TEA Portal, accessed through TEAL and ECOS, is the main hub where you submit, verify, and monitor your certification progress.

Creating and Accessing Your TEAL Account

Begin at the Texas Education Agency (TEA) website. Click the "TEA Login (TEAL)" link, usually located at the upper right corner of the page. If you don't have a TEAL account, select "Request New User Account." Fill out the registration form with your legal name, a unique personal email address, and create a password that meets the security requirements displayed on the form. Use an email address you check regularly, as TEA will send crucial alerts to it.

As you finish the registration process, you'll receive two emails — one with a verification link and another with an activation code. Click the verification link, paste in your code, and set up your security questions. Write down your username and password for later use, as you'll need them every time you visit the portal. If you already have a TEAL account, simply log in using your existing credentials.

Navigating to ECOS in the TEAL Dashboard

Once logged in, you'll see the TEAL dashboard. Look for the "Applications" section, where you'll find "Educator Certification Online System (ECOS)." Click "ECOS for Educators." If ECOS isn't listed, click "Add Access" and select ECOS, then submit the access request. After approval (typically within 24 hours), ECOS will appear next time you log in (2025).

Updating Personal Profile Information

Inside ECOS, the first screen you see will be your personal profile. Review your details — including name, date of birth, and contact information — for accuracy. Click "Edit" next to any item that needs updating. For legal name changes, you may need supporting documentation. Always check that your email and mailing address are up-to-date, since TEA sends critical notices about your application status to these addresses.

Choosing the Correct Certificate Type

Move to the "Applications" tab and select "Standard Certificate Application." A drop-down menu will prompt you to pick the certificate area that matches your teaching field, such as "EC–6," "4–8 Math," or special education. Ensure your selection matches your educator preparation program recommendation. If unsure, consult your program advisor before proceeding. Choosing the wrong type can cause processing delays or application rejection.

Reviewing the Educator Code of Ethics

Before you can submit your application, you must review and acknowledge the Texas Educator Code of Ethics. The system will display the Code for your review. Click the "Acknowledge" button after reading the document. This step is required to demonstrate your understanding of professional expectations. Expect a confirmation banner or pop-up displaying "Acknowledgement Received" after you complete this task.

Uploading Required Documentation

The portal will prompt you to upload supporting documents, such as your official transcripts, test score reports, or alternative certification program certificate. Click "Upload Document," select the file from your device (.pdf or .jpg formats are typically accepted), and then hit "Save." Check that your document appears in the uploaded files list. If a file won't upload, try renaming it without special characters or reducing its file size. Contact TEA technical support if issues persist (Document Display (PURL) | NSCEP | US EPA, 2016).

Verifying Program Recommendations

Your educator preparation program must submit an electronic recommendation through ECOS confirming that you've met all preparation requirements. Under the "Eligibility" or "Recommendations" section, look for the statement "Recommended for certification by [Program Name]." If this is missing after a few days, reach out to your program coordinator, as your application will not process until it's in place.

Understanding and Paying Certification Fees

Once all information is complete, you'll see a balance summary. As of 2025, the initial certification fee for most standard certificates is $78. This fee can be paid by credit card (Visa, Mastercard, Discover) or electronic check. Click "Pay Fees," review the details, and select your payment method. After submitting payment, look for a payment confirmation screen and expect a confirmation email within minutes. Save your receipt for your records.

Saving Progress and Troubleshooting

You can save your application at any point by clicking "Save & Continue Later" at the bottom of a page. To resume an incomplete application, log in, return to ECOS, and select your draft from the dashboard. If your session times out, log in again — the portal may save your last checkpoint. Avoid using browser back buttons, as this can disrupt data entry. If you experience any technical issues, clear your browser cache or switch to a different browser.

Final Review and Preparing for Tracking

Before final submission, use the "Review Application" screen. Double-check every field, ensure all uploaded documents are present, and that fees are paid. Missing information or unchecked steps could delay processing by two or more weeks (2025). Expect a status update banner on your dashboard after you finally submit, which marks your progress towards official certification.

Managing Application Status, Troubleshooting, and Best Practices

After submitting your Texas teacher certification application through the ECOS (Educator Certification Online System) portal, the next two weeks become a period of close monitoring and timely troubleshooting. The Texas Education Agency (TEA) typically processes complete applications within 7 to 14 days, but this timeframe depends heavily on your documentation, responsiveness, and the current workload at TEA (Texas Teacher Certification | State Approved Program, 2024). Understanding how to use the ECOS dashboard and practicing proactive follow-up are crucial for a smooth application experience.

Monitoring Your Application in ECOS

The ECOS portal provides real-time status updates. Begin by logging in daily using your TEAL (TEA Login) credentials. A status bar outlines each stage: "Received," "Under Review," "Pending Documentation," or "Recommended by EPP." Each message signals what's next. For example, "Pending Documentation" suggests your application is missing required papers, while "Under Review" means that your materials are being evaluated. "Recommended by EPP" indicates your Educator Preparation Program has submitted their endorsement for your certification, an essential step for moving forward (Texas Teacher Certification | State Approved Program, 2024).

Always check the notifications area for direct messages from TEA. These may contain requests for additional information or highlight errors in your submission. Promptly responding through the portal avoids unnecessary delays.

Document Tracking and Strategic Submission

Missing or incomplete documents are the most common cause of application holds. To prevent this, use a strategic, methodical approach:

- **Compile a digital folder** labeled with your name and application date. Include scanned transcripts, exam scores, photo ID, EPP recommendation letter, and a saved payment confirmation.
- **Organize your paper documents** in a physical file, attaching a checklist at the front. Cross off each item as you upload it to ECOS.
- **Only use official transcripts** bearing institution seals and signatures; unofficial documents trigger delays.
- **Save the confirmation receipt** after each upload or submission, and take a screenshot of the confirmation screen.

An applicant who submitted an unofficial transcript was moved to "Processing Hold" until they uploaded a sealed, official version. Setting aside a specific date each week to organize and review your documents ensures completeness before each submission step.

Background Check and Fingerprinting

A frequent obstacle is background check delays. Immediately following your application, schedule a fingerprinting appointment through the authorized vendor portal. Bring a government-issued ID and the TEA-provided code to your appointment. Log onto the ECOS system two business days after fingerprinting to confirm receipt of your results. If your background check is listed as "Pending" for more than three days, contact TEA via the messaging tool provided in ECOS (Texas Teacher Certification | State Approved Program, 2024).

If background screening identifies missing records or errors, respond quickly to all TEA inquiries. Example: If the portal notifies you with "Action Required: Additional Information Needed for Background Check," upload the requested documents or clarification through the communication tools in ECOS.

Securing EPP Recommendations and Managing Holds

Certification requires an EPP (Educator Preparation Program) recommendation. You might see a status such as "Pending EPP Recommendation." In this case, email your program's certification officer and provide your TEA ID number and application date. A best practice is to ask your EPP for confirmation after they submit their endorsement to TEA.

Some candidates encounter "Processing Hold: EPP Notified." This message means TEA awaits your EPP's action. Send a courteous reminder to your program and ask if there are issues on their end. Document all correspondence for your records.

Verifying Submission Completeness

An actionable checklist helps you confirm that everything necessary has been submitted:

- Confirm all "Required" ECOS fields are completed.
- Ensure your official transcripts are legible and uploaded in PDF format.
- Check your background check status for a green or "Completed" indicator.
- Verify that payment status lists "Paid" or "Processed." If it says "Unpaid," revisit your fee portal and complete the transaction.
- Obtain written confirmation from your EPP that your recommendation has gone through.

By checking your portal every 48 hours and creating reminder alerts for yourself, you reduce the risk of missed steps.

Responding to TEA Communications

When contacted by TEA for clarification — often flagged as "Request for Correction" or "Missing Information" — respond within 24 hours. Type clear, respectful answers and attach supporting documentation as requested. Keep records of all communications and upload confirmation emails to your digital folder.

Using Support Resources

TEA offers downloadable application checklists and portal guides that can be saved to your desktop or phone. Review these line-by-line before starting your application and again before each submission batch. Use sample forms available from your EPP or the TEA website to double-check formatting and required fields (DAAT List, 2017).

Proactive Measures for Success

Start fingerprinting and background checks the moment your application is in progress. Always keep your TEA contact details up-to-date — missed emails can cause significant setbacks.

Confirm each document's acceptance in the ECOS system before marking it off your checklist. By adopting these detailed steps and maintaining open, organized communication with both TEA and your EPP, you'll navigate the monitoring phase with confidence and avoid common pitfalls (Texas Teacher Certification | State Approved Program, 2024; DAAT List, 2017).

Final Thoughts

Now that you have a clear, step-by-step understanding of how to gather your documents, use the TEA portal, and manage every part of your Texas teacher certification application, you're well prepared to take confident action. By staying organized, double-checking details, and keeping open communication with both TEA and your educator preparation program, you can smooth out bumps along the way and avoid common delays. Whether you're just starting your teaching journey, switching careers, or coming from another country, this roadmap gives you the tools to move forward without feeling overwhelmed. With careful attention and persistence, soon you'll be one step closer to stepping into the classroom as a certified teacher.

Chapter 7:
Building Your Teaching Portfolio

Building and Presenting an Outstanding Teaching Portfolio

"How do I show them who I really am as a teacher?" That question keeps coming up, whether you're just starting out, switching careers, or trying to make sense of a new certification system. It's not just about listing what you've done — it's about telling your story in a way that makes others see your passion, skills, and potential. Building a teaching portfolio isn't like packing a suitcase; it's more like putting together a personal gallery that highlights the moments that matter most in your journey. And when it's time to step into an interview or lead a demonstration lesson, this collection becomes your strongest voice. Knowing how to assemble and present this portfolio can open doors, boost your confidence, and help you stand out in ways that go beyond resumes and test scores. This chapter takes a straightforward look at how to create a portfolio that works for you and prepares you to shine when opportunities come knocking.

Assembling an Effective Teaching Portfolio

A teaching portfolio is more than a collection of classroom documents. It is a tool that showcases instructional skill, professional growth, and readiness for new opportunities. Three core artifact types form the backbone of an effective teaching portfolio: lesson plans, assessments, and student work samples. Each serves a distinct purpose and requires careful curation.

Key Artifacts: Lesson Plans, Assessments, and Student Work

Lesson plans are among the most critical artifacts. They offer direct evidence of instructional design and flexibility. To choose lesson plans for a portfolio, focus on those that highlight a range of teaching approaches, especially differentiation for diverse learners. For example, including a plan that outlines stations for varied readiness levels or integrates ELL support shows an ability to address student needs. A middle school math lesson might detail group tasks for different proficiency levels; an English language arts unit could provide supporting materials for both advanced and struggling readers. Select plans that required adaptation or collaboration, and consider including versions with teacher notes showing revision after implementation.

Assessment examples should demonstrate both formative and summative strategies. Choose assessments that align with lesson objectives and measure essential learning outcomes. A formative assessment could be an exit ticket with analysis of student responses and notes about instructional adjustments. For summative examples, include a unit test or project rubric, plus before-and-after samples if modifications improved clarity or fairness. For instance, an original essay rubric might have unclear criteria, while the revised version includes specific descriptors and a student feedback section. If digital platforms were used, screenshots from apps like Google Forms or Socrative, annotated with reflection on student performance, provide further evidence of evaluation skills.

Student work samples are direct proof of teaching effectiveness. Select pieces that align with showcased lesson plans or assessments. This could be a writing sample from a unit on persuasive essays, accompanied by the draft, final version, and your written feedback. Where privacy is a concern, remove identifying information and use pseudonyms. Secure permissions when needed, and follow school guidelines on sharing student work (Portfolios, n.d.).

Artifact Selection: Guidelines and Examples

When choosing lesson plans, prioritize those demonstrating differentiation and reflective revision. Annotate each plan, briefly explaining instructional choices and what changed after classroom application. Use lesson plans that successfully incorporated feedback from supervisors or mentors, showing professional growth and receptiveness.

For assessment selection, provide evidence of more than simple grading. Include rubrics that explain expectations and support self-assessment. Pair these with samples of feedback written to students, highlighting specific strengths and next steps. If using digital tools, export result summaries from platforms like Edpuzzle or Nearpod and add reflective notes about trends in student understanding.

For student work, use anonymized samples that correlate directly to lesson plans and assessments. If possible, show a progression — an initial rough draft and a polished final version. Images of group projects, coded with initials, can illustrate collaborative learning. Always protect student identity by removing names and photos unless there is explicit consent (Portfolios, n.d.).

Format Considerations: Digital vs. Physical Portfolios

Both digital and physical portfolios have distinct advantages. A digital portfolio offers easy access, multimedia integration, and simple updating. Platforms such as Google Sites, Wix, and Seesaw allow embedding lesson plans, videos of teaching, and interactive elements like voice-over reflections. Digital portfolios are ideal for sharing with certifying bodies, interview committees, or as ongoing professional development tools. Features like password protection and user analytics add layers of security and insight (Faculty Perceptions of Electronic Portfolios in a Teacher Education Program – CITE Journal, 2016).

Physical portfolios can stand out in face-to-face interviews. They offer a tactile experience, allowing interviewers to flip through sturdy binders with dividers, tabs, and color copies of student work. High print quality and thoughtful arrangement signal attention to presentation. Tangible portfolios also avoid technical issues like connectivity problems, ensuring reliable access in any setting.

Hybrid solutions combine the accessibility of digital formats with the presence of physical ones. For example, print a QR code inside a binder to link directly to a digital portfolio with videos or interactive elements.

Practical Tips for Organization and Presentation

Organizing a portfolio depends on audience and purpose. Structure artifacts chronologically to showcase growth, or thematically to highlight skill areas such as classroom management or technology integration. For digital formats, use clear file naming conventions (e.g., "Grade5_Math_Differentiation_LessonPlan.docx") and folders labeled by topic or skill.

Presentation matters. Use consistent fonts, color schemes, and layouts for both digital and printed materials. Include a table of contents or index. Make sure all hyperlinks and digital media work correctly. Add brief introductions or captions for each section, explaining the context and your role. Accessibility is crucial: use large, readable text, and include alternative text for images and screen reader compatibility where possible.

Well-chosen artifacts and thoughtful format decisions not only strengthen a portfolio's impact during hiring and certification but also lay the foundation for ongoing refinement, reflection, and professional growth as new experiences are added (Portfolios, n.d.; Faculty Perceptions of

Electronic Portfolios in a Teacher Education Program — CITE Journal, 2016).

Reflecting and Updating for Professional Growth

Teaching portfolios serve as living documents that mirror a teacher's growth and values over time. Adaptability, honesty, and self-awareness are at the core of a compelling portfolio, especially within the reflective sections and through regular updates. These two practices work together to guide authentic professional development and ensure that portfolios remain genuine tools for showcasing teaching competence.

Reflective Statements: Telling a Professional Story

A reflective statement isn't just a summary of your career or a list of your responsibilities. It's a clear, thoughtful narrative connecting your teaching philosophy to your daily practice — an opportunity to show, with concrete examples, how you approach education and why those beliefs matter. Start by describing your teaching philosophy in plain language. For instance, you might write, "I believe every child learns differently, so I design lessons that offer multiple ways for students to engage with content." This is direct and shows a commitment to differentiation.

It helps to anchor your values in specific classroom moments. If your philosophy centers around active participation, describe a unit where you used group debates, student-led inquiry, or hands-on activities. Maybe you noticed that a quiet student contributed more during a visual arts project. Instead of simply stating, "I encourage participation," detail how "Sarah, a reserved student, led her group's mural project, illustrating that incorporating art into lessons can help quieter students express themselves" (Teacher, 2024). This not only ties your experience to your stated philosophy but demonstrates your ability to observe and respond to student needs in an authentic way.

The most effective reflective statements analyze professional growth, not just classroom outcomes. A strong reflection might look like: "During my first semester, I struggled to manage time during group projects. After attending a workshop on collaborative learning, I restructured my lessons to include time checkpoints and clear roles, which improved both participation and project completion rates" (Teaching Portfolio Development | Michael v. Drake Institute for Teaching and Learning, 2024). Weak reflective writing sticks to generalities, like "Group projects are sometimes challenging, and I am working to get better." The strong example lays out a problem, explains the actions taken, and describes the impact — all in connection with continued professional development.

Artifacts included in your portfolio become more valuable when you reference them directly in reflective writing. For example, when you discuss your adoption of digital formative assessments, point to a specific student work sample or assessment data included in your portfolio. "I introduced weekly online quizzes and used the results to identify learning gaps, as shown in the assessment data included in my portfolio" (Teacher, 2024). This approach grounds your reflection in real evidence and demonstrates intentional practice.

Portfolio Maintenance: Keeping Content Current and Relevant

An effective teaching portfolio grows as your career evolves — it isn't a static archive. The key to maintaining a strong portfolio lies in careful selection, ongoing updates, and the thoughtful inclusion of feedback. First, apply clear criteria for what stays and what goes. Each item should be recent, reflect your current values and abilities, and align with the type of job you're seeking. Ask yourself: Does this artifact represent my teaching style? Is it directly connected to my reflective statement or philosophy? Can I use this to discuss student growth or instructional change? Materials that feel outdated, duplicate other entries, or don't tie into your current teaching context should be removed (Teaching Portfolio Development | Michael v. Drake Institute for Teaching and Learning, 2024).

Establish a routine for reviewing your portfolio. Many successful educators set a schedule — reviewing content at the end of each semester or after completing major projects. This habit allows you to add new lesson plans, student feedback, and professional development certificates while removing less relevant materials. It can be helpful to keep a digital version of your portfolio for easy ongoing edits. Online platforms even offer templates so you can quickly reorganize or substitute new content (Teacher, 2024).

Mentor and peer feedback are powerful tools for growth and improvement. When a colleague reviews your reflective statement or interviews you as practice, listen for suggestions about clarity, depth, or missing evidence. For example, your mentor might notice a section is thin on details about how you support struggling learners. Use their input to revise your narrative or add specific, relevant artifacts. Gathering feedback is as important as acting on it — deliberately review your portfolio with trusted mentors or instructional leaders and make updating a collaborative, ongoing process (Teacher, 2024).

Reflection and updates serve as both mirrors and road maps. As you look back on your journey and tweak your portfolio, you identify your strengths and areas for growth — helping you become a more responsive, reflective educator. Making reflection and maintenance a habit ensures that your portfolio never feels out of date. It will always tell your unique story, highlight your dedication to students, and position you for opportunities in any teaching environment (Teaching Portfolio Development | Michael v. Drake Institute for Teaching and Learning, 2024; Teacher, 2024).

Excelling in Interviews and Demonstration Lessons

Preparing for the interview is the moment when all your reflective portfolio work comes to life. The questions you'll face are designed to uncover your teaching approach, interpersonal skills, and professional values. By referencing your best portfolio pieces, reflective statements, and concrete experiences, you can turn interviews and demonstration lessons into clear demonstrations of your readiness for the classroom.

Structuring Interview Responses

Begin by developing frameworks for common classroom management scenarios. First, for a student exhibiting off-task behavior, use a three-step response: observe quietly, approach the student for a private check-in, and offer a corrective strategy based on established class norms. When responding, highlight a portfolio artifact such as your classroom management plan: "In my portfolio, you'll see my proactive approach, including individualized goal tracking." Next, for recurring disruptions, mention your restorative practices: describe collaborative problem-solving with the student, communicate expectations, and follow up with documented progress — a social contract included in your portfolio reinforces your consistency. Third, for a whole-class escalation, outline your calm redirection strategy, guided discussion, and group reflection activity, making reference to reflection notes and feedback samples in your documentation (Common Teacher Interview Questions and Preparation Tips, 2023).

For curriculum planning challenges, anticipate questions about adapting to limited resources. Explain how you identified gaps using formative assessments, sourced open educational materials, and differentiated tasks — connect this to lesson modifications in your portfolio.

When asked about aligning units to standards, describe mapping objectives, creating backward design outlines, and gathering student work samples — a scanned unit overview with annotations provides tangible evidence.

Clear communication with parents is essential. If asked how you'd handle a concerned parent email, outline a four-step protocol: acknowledge their concern, share factual classroom data, schedule a phone call, and follow up with action steps — reference a correspondence log or communication template from your portfolio. For a difficult discussion about academic struggles, describe how you collaborate on goal setting, provide concrete examples of student progress, and maintain regular updates — use anonymized progress reports as supporting artifacts.

Professional collaboration often surfaces in interviews. Use a recent co-teaching example: reference goal-setting for a shared project, tracking outcomes using defined metrics (such as increased student engagement rates or assessment improvement), and documenting the results in your portfolio's collaboration section (Chapter 1: High Impact Recruitment Strategies, n.d.).

Demonstration Lesson Planning

A demonstration lesson is your opportunity to showcase instructional skill and student engagement. Start with a pre-lesson checklist: review the supervising teacher's objectives, prepare adaptable materials, check technology, and gather portfolio lesson plans for reference. A recommended timing breakdown for 30 minutes is: introduction and lesson objective (5 minutes), core activity (15 minutes), formative assessment (5 minutes), and closure with reflection (5 minutes).

Different grade levels require adapted engagement strategies. For elementary students, use hands-on manipulatives or movement breaks; for older students, incorporate peer discussions or real-world scenarios. Short, quick checks (exit tickets or hand signals) let you demonstrate assessment strategies, while portfolio samples of formative assessments provide visible proof.

Prepare backup plans in case of technical issues or time constraints. Bring printed materials, simplify activities for quicker pacing, and mention how you've adapted on the fly in previous teaching contexts — with visual aids or brief portfolio notes highlighting flexibility.

Developing Presentation Skills

Practice voice modulation by reading lesson segments aloud, recording, and adjusting pitch for emphasis. Try projecting your voice in an empty classroom, then practice lowering it for instructions. To prepare for the interview setting, monitor your posture — stand tall, avoid closed gestures, and maintain gentle but steady eye contact. Mimic these behaviors in front of a mirror or with a trusted peer and compare them to professional standards found in your portfolio's video reflections.

Dress professionally, matching your attire to the school culture. Choose classic options for elementary settings or business-casual for secondary schools, ensuring comfort as well as professionalism. Jot down wardrobe plans and keep photos in your portfolio for easy reference before interviews.

To manage nerves, develop a confidence routine: breathe deeply, visualize a positive outcome, and rehearse answers aloud. Rate your anxiety after each practice and chart your progress as a self-assessment tool, just as you've tracked learning growth in your portfolio.

Follow-Up Protocol

After the interview, send a concise, appreciative email. Begin by thanking the panel for specific conversations (such as discussion about student engagement or the school's mentorship culture), and reference key artifacts or stories you shared from your portfolio. Maintain a professional tone and reiterate your excitement for the opportunity, making sure to send follow-up communication within 24 hours. Use clear subject lines and sign-offs, and avoid overly personal language. Mentioning how your documented experience in a particular area aligns with school initiatives, as discussed in the interview, helps to reinforce your professionalism and cohesion throughout the process (Common Teacher Interview Questions and Preparation Tips, 2023).

These strategies, rooted in intentional portfolio development, equip candidates to clearly articulate their experience, showcase meaningful artifacts, and present themselves as capable, reflective educators ready for classroom challenges (Chapter 1: High Impact Recruitment Strategies, n.d.). Self-assess after mock interviews by reviewing checklists and seeking feedback, ensuring you are fully prepared to step confidently into your new teaching role.

Bringing It All Together

Now that you understand how to build a strong teaching portfolio and prepare thoughtfully for interviews and demonstration lessons, you're well on your way to showing your true potential as an educator. By carefully selecting meaningful artifacts, reflecting on your growth, and practicing clear communication, you can confidently navigate the certification process and job search — no matter your background or experience level.

Remember, this portfolio isn't just a requirement; it's your story of dedication, skill, and readiness to make a difference in the classroom. With these tools and strategies in hand, you're ready to take the next step toward a rewarding teaching career.

Chapter 8:
Beyond Certification: Lifelong Learning and Professional Development

The Importance of Ongoing Professional Development for Teachers

Imagine stepping into your first teaching job full of hope and energy, only to realize that earning your initial certificate is just the beginning. Unlike many professions where a license lasts a lifetime, teaching requires constant renewal — not just paperwork, but real learning to keep up with changes in education, technology, and student needs. This ongoing process can feel overwhelming, especially if you're new or changing careers, but it also opens doors to growth and opportunities you might never have expected. Understanding how professional development works, why it matters, and what options you have will help you stay on track, keep your skills sharp, and build a successful career that evolves alongside the classroom.

Mandatory Continuing Education Essentials

In every state, teachers must complete continuing education to keep their teaching credentials active. Continuing Education Units (CEUs) act as a standardized measurement for hours spent learning after earning initial certification. One CEU typically represents ten hours of instruction in an accredited professional development activity. Approved CEU activities are broad, ranging from college coursework to workshops, educational conferences, online modules, and certificate renewal courses. For example, in Mississippi, teachers must renew their certificates every five years by earning CEUs, college credits, or national board certifications. These CEUs must come from an accredited body, such as a university continuing education office or a college-approved provider (Continuing Education Units (CEUs) – Educator Licensure, 2024).

Most states establish both activity guidelines and the number of CEUs needed for renewal. North Carolina, for example, may require different professional development hours depending on the focus or skill area, while Texas demands 150 continuing professional education (CPE) hours every five years, which equates to 15 hours a year, with topic areas that can include technology training, special education, or ethics. Some states, like Oregon, require educators to earn 25 professional development units (PDUs) annually, and college credits can be converted to a set number of PDUs for this purpose (Professional Development Requirements by State for Education, 2025).

CESs are always tightly linked to state standards and priorities. Activities that qualify for CEUs are usually designed to align with state and district education goals, ensuring that teachers update their skills in areas most relevant to student achievement. For instance, Texas includes CPE hours specifically for training in educating students with disabilities, promoting consistent teacher growth in targeted topics (Professional Development Requirements by State for Education, 2025). Common activities approved for CEU credits include attending teacher workshops on literacy instruction, taking graduate-level courses in classroom management, or participating in district-led technology integration seminars.

Typical Credential Renewal Process

Credential renewal cycles tend to fall between three and five years in most states, reinforcing the need for ongoing learning. Periodically requiring renewal ensures teacher knowledge remains current and classroom practices reflect ongoing research and innovations. Mississippi uses a straightforward five-year license period that is reset each time a teacher demonstrates completion of required CEUs or college coursework (Continuing Education Units (CEUs) – Educator Licensure, 2024). Louisiana, South Dakota, and South Carolina also use similar five-year renewal systems, with specifics varying based on educator roles and employment status (Professional Development Requirements by State for Education, 2025).

Failure to comply with credential renewal requirements can lead to certificate suspension, non-renewal, or even revocation in more severe cases. This can have a direct effect on a teacher's employment status, sometimes resulting in job loss until the required professional development is completed and documentation is re-submitted. Therefore, timely credential maintenance is both a professional necessity and a legal requirement in education.

Professional Development Activities

Professional learning is available in a variety of forms, often tailored to individual or school-level needs. These include in-person and virtual workshops, university or college credit classes, district-provided in-service training, and curriculum-specific bootcamps. Common formats are one- or two-day workshops, semester-long college courses, or ongoing learning communities that meet periodically throughout the year.

School districts play a key role in providing accessible and focused development opportunities. Districts may offer summer institutes, afterschool workshops, and required in-person or online training days. Rhode Island's 100 Professional Learning Units (PLUs) requirement, for example, encourages participation in a range of workshops and conferences, often coordinated at the district level to support district and state priorities (Professional Development Requirements by State for Education, 2025).

Successful district programs often include mentoring for new teachers, specialized seminars on classroom management, or evidence-based training in reading instruction. Some states also encourage teachers to earn renewal credits by engaging in research projects, presenting at conferences, or publishing articles in professional journals, offering a choice of activities to meet the needs of a diverse teaching workforce.

Documentation Requirements

Accurate, organized documentation is essential for license renewal. Teachers must keep detailed records of their completed CEUs, which may include certificates of attendance, transcripts, or verified logs of participation in district workshops. In many states, teachers must submit official forms and supporting documents before their license expiration date. Some districts require forms with supervisor signatures or unique course codes for each learning activity.

Many states and school districts use online systems to track and verify CEUs, including secure digital portals and credentialing management platforms. These systems allow teachers to upload proof of completion, monitor progress toward renewal, and ensure all required documentation is in order. Practical tips include storing digital copies of certificates, maintaining a running list of all professional development activities, and confirming activity approval in advance. Careful documentation not only protects teachers during audits but also encourages intentional participation in a broad range of learning activities that support career growth and classroom effectiveness (Continuing Education Units (CEUs) – Educator Licensure, 2024; Professional Development Requirements by State for Education, 2025).

Maintaining Status and Documentation

Teachers have a wide range of professional development options designed to help them meet state and district renewal requirements while boosting their day-to-day effectiveness. Many districts and states require educators to earn Continuing Education Units (CEUs) or clock hours to maintain their teaching credentials. Teachers often encounter diverse courses, such as classroom management workshops, technology integration sessions, and subject matter refreshers, all tailored to meet current educational needs (NACC - Online Training Center, 2024).

Professional development activities can include online courses covering instructional planning, adaptive learning, or effective teaching strategies. For example, a "Mobile Technology in the Classroom" workshop might walk educators through hands-on exercises for using tablets, smartphones, and apps to engage students and manage assignments. These kinds of technology-focused sessions help teachers weave modern tools into learning experiences, making lessons more interactive and relevant (An Error Has Occurred, 2025). Other popular choices include peer review seminars or goal-setting courses, which encourage educators to reflect and build on their instructional practices.

School districts frequently partner with local colleges, national training centers, and even software companies to ensure the training aligns closely with classroom realities. Districts may organize targeted summer institutes or after-school workshops, bringing in experts on specific topics, such as integrating Universal Design for Learning or managing accelerated learning environments (NACC - Online Training Center, 2024). Educators often join department-wide or building-wide sessions together, which encourages collaboration and advances consistent teaching approaches.

When selecting professional development, teachers are advised to verify whether a course or workshop is approved for CEU credit. Typically, activities that request active participation or require the completion of coursework — like lesson plan design, classroom simulations, or peer observation — meet district or state credit guidelines. Reviewing course descriptions for clear learning objectives, qualified instructors, and practical classroom applications helps ensure the activity is both relevant and high quality. Reading feedback from past participants and checking if the training is on the state's approved list can also prevent wasted time on non-credit experiences (An Error Has Occurred, 2025).

A typical professional development experience might look like this: On a scheduled in-service day, a group of teachers gathers for a five-hour session on behavior management. After signing in, they engage in role-play exercises addressing common classroom disruptions and exchange strategies for redirecting students. At the end, each participant receives a certificate, which specifies the number of training hours completed.

Proper documentation of CEUs is essential. Teachers must keep thorough records as proof for license renewal, audits, or evaluations. The most important records include certificates of completion, sign-in sheets from each session, official transcripts for accredited courses, and any feedback forms required by the district or state. Many trainers now supply digital certificates, while in-person events use paper documentation.

Efficient record-keeping begins at the workshop or course itself. Teachers make sure their full name, educator ID, and the session's date are clearly listed on every sign-in sheet. When a certificate or attendance log is issued, it is best to scan the document immediately and upload it to a secure digital folder. Some school districts provide online tracking portals, where educators can log in, upload certificates, record course details, and view their

CEU history over the years (NACC - Online Training Center, 2024). These digital systems are popular because they make it easy to organize, search, and retrieve records during an audit.

Teachers without district-provided systems often use spreadsheets or cloud storage solutions, such as Google Drive or Dropbox, to sort certificates by school year or renewal cycle. For example, after completing a "Partnering with Parents" workshop, a teacher might save the certificate as "2024_Partnering_with_Parents_CEU.pdf" in a folder labeled "PD_2024." Adding notes about the session's topic, provider, and number of hours can prevent confusion later.

For audit preparation, best practices include keeping originals and digital backups, maintaining a simple checklist of required renewal hours, and updating records after each session. Teachers usually conduct a mid-year review to check if they are on track with their renewal requirements. When notified of an upcoming audit, gathering certificates, transcripts, and official forms into one easily accessible location helps streamline the process. Labeling each file with course title, date, and credit earned is an effective way to demonstrate compliance quickly.

Staying organized with systematic documentation protects teachers during audits. It also enables them to reflect on their growth and plan future professional development goals. This level of accountability helps teachers show their ongoing commitment to learning and ensures they are always prepared for state or district review.

Voluntary Professional Growth Pathways

Ambitious teachers seeking to go beyond what is required can take advantage of several voluntary professional development options that offer concrete benefits both inside and outside the classroom. National Board Certification, advanced academic degrees, participation in education conferences, and regular engagement with new research all provide pathways for educators to advance their skills, boost their careers, and improve student outcomes.

National Board Certification

Teachers in K-12 settings can pursue National Board Certification to earn one of the highest recognitions in the profession. This advanced, voluntary certificate sets teachers on a multi-year journey with four key components: a content knowledge assessment delivered by computer, submission of student work with reflective commentary to demonstrate differentiation in instruction, a teaching and learning portfolio requiring classroom video and analysis, and evidence showing effective and reflective practice in one's school and local community (National Board Certification, 2025). While teachers may opt to complete all four parts in one year, many spread the workload over two or three years for a more manageable balance alongside regular teaching duties. Candidates typically spend dozens of hours outside of contract time preparing materials, recording lessons, and editing written commentary.

The effort is rewarded in many ways. National Board Certified Teachers (NBCTs) report increased recognition, expanded leadership opportunities, and regular mentorship roles supporting other educators (National Board Certification, 2025). In West Virginia, teachers earn salary bonuses and can get program fees reimbursed. NBCTs' classrooms often show higher student achievement and a greater culture of collaborative improvement (National Board Certification, 2025). For instance, a teacher certified in Literacy: Reading-Language Arts may develop units that more effectively meet diverse literacy needs, analyze student work with stronger precision, and inspire instructional changes that ripple across grade-level teams (The Case for National Board Certification: Lived Experiences to

Aspire and Sustain National Board Certification - ProQuest, 2022).

Graduate Education

Building on a bachelor's degree, many teachers pursue advanced degrees to improve their effectiveness and open new career opportunities. Programs include master's degrees in curriculum and instruction, special education, leadership, English as a second language, and content specialties such as mathematics or science. Those looking for leadership or academic research roles may choose a Doctor of Education (Ed.D) or a Doctor of Philosophy (Ph.D) in education. Master's programs typically require 1.5 to 3 years part-time with costs that range widely by institution, but often result in salary increases, eligibility for specialist roles, or access to administration positions. Doctoral programs generally require three to five years with significant time dedicated to research and dissertation work.

The knowledge gained through coursework and research projects equips teachers with advanced understanding of pedagogy, assessment, and leadership. For example, a teacher who completes a master's in educational technology may introduce new digital learning tools district-wide or support colleagues in designing online lessons. The advanced learning often translates into classroom innovation — teachers apply concepts right away, such as differentiated instruction frameworks or new approaches to inclusive education.

Conference Participation

Joining local, national, or subject-specific educational conferences remains a popular way for teachers to stay current and inspired. Events like the National Council of Teachers of Mathematics (NCTM) Annual Meeting, the International Society for Technology in Education (ISTE) Conference, or state reading association conferences offer both in-person and online formats. Conference fees range from $100 to $500 plus travel, but many districts offer support or grants for attendance.

Presenting at a conference — by sharing a classroom innovation, a curriculum project, or research data — builds professional visibility and confidence. Preparing a proposal, crafting a presentation, and interacting with a live audience provide valuable skills. Teachers frequently report that a single conference can add multiple new teaching strategies to their toolkits: after attending a workshop on culturally responsive lesson planning, for example, many educators revise their units to better reflect student backgrounds and experiences.

Research Engagement

Teachers who regularly interact with new educational research stay at the forefront of their field. Subscriptions to journals, memberships in professional organizations, and university partnerships provide access to timely studies about classroom management, learning differences, and effective instructional strategies. Reading one or two research articles per month or participating in a local action research project demands some extra effort but pays off by equipping teachers with evidence-based practices.

Practical steps include joining a statewide reading initiative, implementing intervention strategies found in peer-reviewed journals, or collaborating with nearby colleges on pilot programs. For instance, a teacher inspired by a recent study on formative assessment might revamp unit tests to include more feedback and self-reflection, resulting in measurable gains in student understanding.

Each of these professional development pathways requires an investment of time, energy, and sometimes finances, but the rewards come in the form of personal fulfillment, career advancement, improved teaching quality, and better student outcomes (National Board Certification, 2025; *The Case for National Board Certification: Lived Experiences to Aspire and Sustain National Board Certification* - ProQuest, 2022).

Concluding Thoughts

Now that we understand the importance of ongoing education and professional development, it's clear that maintaining teacher certification goes far beyond earning an initial license.

Whether through required continuing education units, renewing credentials regularly, or seeking extra growth opportunities like advanced degrees and certifications, these steps help teachers stay current, effective, and inspired in their work. Keeping organized records and actively choosing meaningful learning experiences not only meets legal requirements but also opens doors to career advancement and improved teaching skills. For anyone starting or changing careers in education, embracing continuous learning will be a powerful tool to build confidence, adapt to classroom challenges, and create better outcomes for students throughout your teaching journey.

Chapter 9:
Technology, Tools, and Teacher Certification in the 21st Century

The Digital Transformation of Teaching: Skills and Certification for Modern Educators

As a principal I always provided professional development sessions for my staff. At the beginning of each school year I always had to train the staff on various technological aspects from the district. One of the constant phrases I heard mumbled throughout the room was, "Wait, we have to learn how to use what now?" Many of my novice teachers stated that the list of apps and platforms their certification program expected them to master before even stepping into a classroom was long and quite confusing. They stated that It felt overwhelming — like teaching itself was just one part of the job, and suddenly they needed to become a tech expert too.

Whether you're thinking about becoming a teacher, switching careers, or preparing for exams, you might be facing that same surprise. Things have changed, and today's educators need more than just lesson plans — they need digital skills that open new doors in the classroom and beyond.

Years ago, earning your teaching certificate meant mostly studying curriculum and spending hours in student teaching. Now, technology shapes not only how you teach but also how you prove you're ready. From managing online classrooms to protecting student data and creating digital portfolios, modern certification taps into tools and skills no one talked about before. But don't let that discourage you. Like any new skill, learning these digital essentials happens step by step — and each one helps build confidence and flexibility for a teaching career that fits today's world.

If you're new to this journey or coming from a different field, you're not alone. Many people wonder if they can keep up with ever-changing technology or if alternative certification paths make sense. The truth is, there are many options tailored to busy adults, career changers, international educators, and recent grads alike. Understanding the landscape of skills and certification today gives you a clearer path forward — not just for passing tests, but for thriving in classrooms that blend in-person and digital learning.

This chapter invites you to take a look behind the scenes at the tools teachers use daily, the safety measures protecting students online, and the ways certification programs have adapted to prepare educators for the future. It's less about mastering every detail right away and more about stepping confidently into what teaching means now — and how you can shape your own success in a world where education is constantly evolving.

Digital Literacy Concepts and Essential Technology Proficiencies

Modern educators must develop strong digital literacy and technology skills to thrive in the 21st-century classroom. Two key areas lay the foundation for effective technology integration: mastering learning management systems (LMS) and skillfully using educational apps.

Understanding both empowers teachers to organize learning, communicate consistently with students, and provide flexible, student-centered instruction that adapts to diverse needs and shifting learning environments (*Benefits of Integrating Technology in the Classroom*, 2025; *What Is Educational Technology and Why Is It Important?*, 2022).

Learning Management Systems (LMS): Features and Practice

Learning management systems such as Google Classroom and Canvas serve as central hubs for classroom organization. With Google Classroom, teachers create virtual classrooms where students join with a code. Assignments, announcements, resources, and deadlines appear in a clear, chronological stream. Teachers can schedule posts, attach Google Docs for collaborative writing, and embed videos for flipped lessons. Canvas offers course modules for organizing units, quizzes with instant feedback, and rubrics for transparent grading. Discussion boards let students debate topics and reflect on readings.

A middle school science teacher might organize a genetics unit in Canvas by uploading lesson slides into weekly modules, attaching handouts, and posting self-graded quizzes after each lesson. The teacher sets up a discussion board for students to pose questions and consider ethical issues in genetics. At the same time, all assignments and reminders stay visible in the digital calendar, ensuring everyone understands the learning path and expectations. Using these organizational features, the teacher spends less time shuffling papers and more time providing targeted feedback or engaging students in deeper inquiry (*Benefits of Integrating Technology in the Classroom*, 2025).

Communication and Feedback

LMS platforms power communication through built-in messaging, announcement tools, and notification systems. Teachers instantly share updates with students and families. If a student misses a class, the teacher can message resources directly through the LMS and check in on progress. Canvas notifications alert students to new grades, while Google Classroom sends reminders for upcoming assignments right to students' mobile devices.

During group projects, students collaborate in real time through Google Docs, which syncs within the LMS. Teachers can add comments, suggest revisions, and track participation. This seamless communication loop reduces confusion and supports accountability, especially in blended learning environments where in-person time is limited. For English language learners or students who need extra help, this steady feedback helps them stay on track and ask for clarification as needed (*What Is Educational Technology and Why Is It Important?*, 2022).

Enabling Remote and Blended Learning

LMS proficiency proves essential for remote or hybrid teaching. When schools close or pivot online, teachers post all lessons, links, and assessments on the platform. Teachers use recorded video lessons, attach practice quizzes, and hold virtual office hours via built-in conference tools. Students access materials anytime, review instructions, and communicate with teachers no matter where they are. In a rural district, for example, Google Classroom bridges distance so students who lack transportation still attend class, submit work, and join discussions from home. These systems also simplify accommodating absences due to illness or family obligations, maintaining continuity in learning and routine (*Benefits of Integrating Technology in the Classroom*, 2025).

Educational Technology Apps: Engaging Learners and Supporting Diverse Needs

Educational apps give teachers additional tools for reaching various learners. Kahoot! and Quizizz inject game-like elements into review sessions, transforming test prep into friendly competition with points, timers, and leaderboards. Students answer questions on their devices, receive instant feedback, and see progress in real time. This gamification motivates even reluctant learners, turning assessment into a positive, low-pressure experience (What Is Educational Technology and Why Is It Important?, 2022).

For hands-on instruction, a teacher might use Nearpod to create multimedia presentations. Slides combine polls, videos, 3D models, and drawing activities that students access on tablets. In a lesson on ecosystems, students watch an embedded video, annotate food webs, and answer quiz questions in one seamless flow. This interactive approach makes abstract concepts concrete, meeting the needs of visual, kinesthetic, and auditory learners.

Apps like Seesaw enable younger students to record audio reflections, draw diagrams, or snap photos of their work. Teachers can differentiate by assigning extra scaffolding or enrichment activities directly within the app based on student readiness, ensuring every learner progresses at the right pace.

Differentiation and Accessibility

Technology apps provide dynamic support for students with disabilities or unique learning profiles. Speech-to-text functions within platforms support writers who struggle with spelling, while built-in screen readers and color filters help students with visual impairments. For ELLs, audio features and translation tools remove language barriers, creating a more equitable classroom (*Benefits of Integrating Technology in the Classroom*, 2025).

Overcoming Challenges and Building Skills

Teachers often face hurdles such as navigating new interfaces, troubleshooting tech glitches, or adapting lessons on the fly. Tackling just one new feature at a time — such as scheduling assignments or setting up a simple digital quiz — builds confidence. Connecting with other educators through online communities or tutorials helps overcome roadblocks and unlock creative uses for these tools. Mastering core features expands flexibility, boosts engagement, and equips teachers to respond to new challenges, preparing them for a tech-driven educational landscape (*What Is Educational Technology and Why Is It Important?*, 2022).

Cyber Safety, Data Privacy, and Hybrid/Remote Teaching Skills

Technology's integration into classrooms has brought new challenges around cyber safety, especially for teachers managing student information. Federal laws, such as the Family Educational Rights and Privacy Act (FERPA), require educators to safeguard personally identifiable student information. This leads to practical protocols like password-protecting gradebooks, encrypting email attachments containing student data, and strictly limiting access to sensitive databases. When sharing academic records, teachers authenticate recipients' identities and use secure digital platforms that audit data access and changes. For example, a teacher sending an Individualized Education Plan to a special education coordinator would use an encrypted district email and require confirmation upon receipt, following specific school policies for access logs and retention periods. Regular data audits, strong passwords, and multi-factor authentication further fortify these systems, preventing unauthorized access and maintaining compliance with cybersecurity standards (*The Policymaker's Guide to Student Data Privacy – Public Interest Privacy Center*, n.d.; Nayyar & Gupta, 2024).

Teachers model digital citizenship by weaving lessons on online etiquette and privacy directly into their curriculum. In a real-world scenario, a middle school class might analyze digital footprints by Googling common names and discussing what can be discovered about someone's online presence. Another activity involves simulated phishing emails where students learn to identify suspicious links and report cyber incidents. Through role-play, students practice respecting others' privacy — never sharing a classmate's photo online without permission, for instance. Teachers also review Acceptable Use Policies (AUPs) with students, encouraging them to report inappropriate content or cyberbullying without fear of reprisal. These lessons build a culture where students understand what is safe to share, which fosters not only security but also empathy and digital responsibility (Nayyar & Gupta, 2024).

Managing student records in a digital environment calls for clear, repeatable steps. Teachers only collect necessary data, immediately storing files in secure cloud-based systems provided by their district. Each file is labeled according to an organized naming convention and only shared with authorized staff using internal encrypted tools. When parents request access to records, teachers verify identities using multi-step authentication before releasing documents. Old files, once they meet retention requirements, are purged following district protocols, reducing risk from obsolete data. Teachers maintain logs of all record transactions as an auditable trail for compliance purposes (*The Policymaker's Guide to Student Data Privacy – Public Interest Privacy Center*, n.d.).

To educate students about privacy, teachers break down complex topics into age-appropriate lessons. In elementary grades, teachers read stories about fictional characters protecting their private information online. Older students review privacy settings within commonly used apps and evaluate third-party data requests. Teachers create simple privacy pledges, have students sign and display them, and regularly revisit these commitments. They also use scenarios — such as posting a group project online — to prompt class discussions around what should and shouldn't be shared. Sample privacy policies, displayed both on classroom websites and sent home to parents, outline how digital assignments, photos, and communications are handled.

These policies spell out that teachers will never post students' names alongside photos, and all online platforms used must meet district privacy standards (Nayyar & Gupta, 2024).

Hybrid classrooms require balancing the needs of in-person and remote students. Teachers employ digital whiteboards, like Jamboard or Padlet, allowing real-time collaboration for all students. To manage participation, interactive polls and chat tools are used so remote learners can contribute alongside classmates in the room. Rotating responsibilities, such as having students lead a virtual discussion or summarize in-person debates, ensures engagement across both groups. Teachers set clear norms — like muting microphones, using hand-raise functions, and respecting digital etiquette — to create a unified classroom environment despite physical separation (*The Policymaker's Guide to Student Data Privacy – Public Interest Privacy Center*, n.d.).

Consistent communication is vital in these blended settings. Teachers utilize centralized learning management systems (LMS) such as Google Classroom to post assignments, feedback, and announcements, maintaining parity for all learners. Weekly check-ins — through video calls or discussion boards — allow teachers to monitor student well-being, address questions, and adapt to individual needs. Hybrid lessons often feature videos paired with live discussions, discussion forums for asynchronous engagement, and project-based tasks where student teams combine virtual and face-to-face collaboration (Nayyar & Gupta, 2024).

Remote teaching benefits from tools that make learning interactive even when students are not online simultaneously. Teachers develop brief, engaging videos explaining core concepts, followed by interactive quizzes using platforms like Kahoot! or Edpuzzle. Self-paced learning modules allow students to navigate content at their own speed, while collaborative documents in Google Workspace help maintain group projects. Participation is upheld through regular feedback and clear checkpoints, keeping students motivated and connected to the class. Effective remote assessment might combine timed online quizzes, digital portfolios of student work, or reflective journals submitted via the LMS, each supporting fair evaluation and academic honesty (*The Policymaker's Guide to Student Data Privacy – Public Interest Privacy Center*, n.d.; Nayyar & Gupta, 2024).

Evolving Teacher Certification Processes Influenced by Technology

Seeking teacher certification looks very different today than it did just a decade ago. With the rise of technology, most states now recognize accredited online educator preparation programs, allowing candidates to complete their coursework and fieldwork from anywhere. For example, Western Governors University is a well-known provider of fully online teacher preparation that satisfies licensure requirements across multiple states. These programs follow the same rigorous standards as campus-based pathways, including supervised student teaching, regular feedback, and comprehensive exams. Quality assurance comes from both internal controls — like integrated assessments and instructor oversight — and external factors such as CAEP accreditation, state education department audits, and candidate performance on standardized licensure tests. The flexible pacing of online courses helps career changers and working adults fit their studies around family and job commitments, while multimedia learning resources and interactive simulations enable practical skill-building in virtual environments (Stavermann, 2024).

Online certification programs often encourage active engagement. Some require synchronous video participation during discussion-based lessons, while others use virtual reality classrooms to simulate real-life student interactions. These experiences prepare future teachers for classrooms that are increasingly blended or fully digital. Diverse cohorts add to the richness: candidates collaborate with peers from across the country and even around the globe, which builds digital communication skills essential for today's classrooms. States like Texas and Florida actively promote virtual preparation pathways, recognizing their potential for reaching candidates in rural areas or those juggling multiple responsibilities.

A significant change brought on by digital transformation is the expectation for teachers to submit digital portfolios as part of their certification process. Instead of only turning in lesson plans and written reflections, candidates now assemble online portfolios featuring classroom video clips, interactive lesson records, screencasts, and digital student work samples. For example, Edthena and GoReact are two platforms allowing teacher candidates to capture teaching segments, annotate them, and receive feedback from mentors. Digital portfolios demonstrate how teachers apply instructional strategies and adapt lessons for diverse learners. Rubrics assess candidates on specific competencies, such as classroom management and technology integration, reflecting current state standards.

Digital portfolio requirements also streamline the certification workflow for state departments and hiring districts. Review committees can quickly view teaching samples, scan reflections, and check for growth over time using tagged evidence. It's much easier for new teachers to update digital work samples through the year, creating an evolving record of professional development and lesson improvement. For career changers, portfolios highlight transferable skills, show adaptability, and provide a real sense of readiness for different teaching contexts (Stavermann, 2024).

AI and automated assessment tools are becoming a common part of candidate evaluation. These technologies analyze teaching videos and written reflections for demonstration of state teaching standards. Tools like TeachFX, for example, process classroom audio and provide reports on teacher talk time, questioning patterns, and wait time, offering specific, data-driven feedback. In some certification programs, automated essay scoring supports supervisor grading, giving both teachers and administrators near-instant responses on candidate performance against rubrics.

However, while the advantages include speed, consistency, and ongoing support, there are ethical considerations about bias in algorithms and privacy of recorded materials. AI can efficiently spot patterns and automate routine reviews but still needs human oversight.

Instructor involvement ensures nuanced understanding and fair evaluation, recognizing context that an automated system might miss (*What Are Impact of AI Integration in Educator Professional Development? | ResearchGate*, 2025).

None of these changes matter if teachers aren't equipped to adapt. Modern certification programs embed professional development modules focused on technology use. Some schools partner with edtech companies to offer micro-credential badges in areas like digital classroom management, formative assessment apps, or universal design for learning. Networking is another adaptation strategy. Through platforms such as Edmodo and proprietary program communities, aspiring educators exchange tips, troubleshoot tech, and build mentoring relationships regardless of physical location. Many online certification pathways provide structured mentorship, pairing candidates with experienced educators who guide them through digital lesson planning and classroom tech integration.

Strong technology integration isn't just a program requirement — it's a lived expectation. Teachers demonstrate flexibility by using collaborative tools like Google Workspace, experiment with AI-driven adaptive learning platforms, and explore online formative assessment systems such as Kahoot! or Quizizz. State standards now often require documented competence in these areas as part of initial and ongoing certification reviews. While challenges exist — like ensuring equitable access to technology, addressing varying levels of digital literacy, and protecting data privacy — the overall trend shows that online programs and digital portfolios are widening access, personalizing preparation, and creating more future-ready teachers (Stavermann, 2024; *What Are Impact of AI Integration in Educator Professional Development? | ResearchGate*, 2025).

Wrapping Up

Now that we understand the essential technology skills educators need and how these tools are shaping teacher certification, it's clear that embracing digital literacy, cyber safety, and adaptability is key to success in today's teaching world. Whether you're new to the profession, switching careers, or navigating certification from abroad, becoming comfortable with online learning platforms, educational apps, and digital portfolios will help you stand out and meet evolving standards. As technology continues to transform classrooms and certification processes, staying curious and open to new methods will prepare you not just to earn your credential, but to thrive as a confident, flexible educator ready for whatever the future of teaching brings.

Chapter 10:
Professional Attire

Professional Appearance in Educational Settings

Have you ever stopped to think about how much your appearance can influence the way others see you in an educational setting? How does the way a teacher dresses affect the respect and trust they receive from students, parents, and coworkers? And what does it really mean to look professional as an educator without losing comfort or personal style? These are questions many new teachers and career changers face as they step into their classrooms for the first time.

Understanding the balance between professionalism, practicality, and individuality might seem tricky at first, but it's a skill that can be learned and mastered. This chapter will help you explore these ideas and find your own path to presenting yourself with confidence and credibility every day.

Foundations of Professional Attire

Expectations, Wardrobe Essentials, and Practical Challenges

Students, families, and colleagues all notice a teacher's professional appearance before any words are spoken. The way a teacher dresses often guides first impressions, setting a tone that may help or hinder relationship-building in a school environment. A carefully chosen outfit can show readiness, reliability, and respect for the role's responsibilities, while distracting or overly casual clothes might raise questions about dedication or authority. Imagine a new teacher who enters the classroom wearing tidy slacks and a collared shirt. This combination blends respect for workplace standards with a friendly presence, helping students know what to expect from the very start. In contrast, a teacher's first day appearance in faded jeans and a graphic tee could blur boundaries, making classroom management and earning respect much harder. When meeting parents, such as during conferences or open houses, polished attire communicates preparedness and signals that they can trust their child's education to a caring professional.

    Wardrobe choices for teachers go far beyond personal style. Every school or district sets expectations for how staff should present themselves. These guidelines may appear in staff handbooks or be shared verbally during orientation. Written dress codes typically list rules on items like jeans, t-shirts, athletic wear, or shoes. For example, a suburban district handbook may ban denim and require closed-toed shoes, while a charter school might allow neat sneakers paired with a school-branded polo. But even with official policies, much of the real decision-making happens through informal cues. Teachers new to a school often watch experienced colleagues and see which clothing choices are accepted.

    Expectations can shift across different types of schools. In some private or religiously-affiliated campuses, teachers will often wear business attire every day, including jackets, skirts, or button-up shirts. On the other hand, rural elementary teachers may regularly choose dark jeans, comfortable sweaters, and boots — viewed as both practical and professional in that setting.

    Urban high schools might encourage more formal clothes to reflect the student population's own dress standards or respond to family expectations. Consider the story of a teacher who arrived in a new city school for an interview: seeing every staff member in jackets and dress shoes, they understood that this was the norm and adjusted their wardrobe accordingly. Community standards make a difference, too. Teachers working in communities that value tradition may face greater expectation for conservative, understated dress, while creative campuses sometimes support colorful or less conventional choices.

Teachers have to balance professionalism, comfort, and practicality. Clothing needs change depending on classroom activities and student age. When teaching music, art, or physical education, being able to move easily matters. A kindergarten teacher helping tie shoelaces or organize play needs sleeves out of the way and shoes made for standing. Often, professional attire falls into three categories:

Types of Attire in Schools

Professional

- Suits or blazers
- Dress pants or knee-length skirts
- Button-up shirts or blouses
- Dress shoes or loafers

Business Casual

- Khakis or tailored pants
- Simple dresses or skirts
- Collared shirts, sweaters, or neat tops
- Clean flats or moderate-heeled shoes

Casual (where permitted)

- Neat jeans with polos or cardigans
- School spirit wear (on designated days)
- Athletic shoes (in gym class or on field trips)

Teachers should shop mindfully to build a wardrobe that fits these categories. Shopping end-of-season sales, browsing thrift stores, or swapping with colleagues can keep costs lower. Versatile pieces — a neutral blazer or comfortable black pants — make mixing and matching outfits easier without spending much. Choosing wrinkle-free fabrics and layering options helps handle unexpected classroom events or temperature swings.

Outfit needs shift by activity. For everyday teaching, a teacher might choose dress pants and a sweater when in front of the class. For parent events, switching to a blazer or statement necklace adds a formal touch. Faculty meetings may lean toward business casual, while leading a science fair might mean dressing in machine-washable clothes. During field trips or recess, even the strictest dress codes make exceptions for hats, sun-protective gear, or sturdy shoes.

Weather often shapes what teachers wear. In regions with cold winters, layering is key. Fleece-lined tights under dresses and thick cardigans keep teachers comfortable during outdoor duties. Hot climates demand breathable fabrics and moisture-wicking shirts. Carrying a spare shirt or stain stick helps if spills or accidents occur during lunch supervision or art class.

Dressing professionally means staying aware of cultural differences. Teachers serving multicultural communities can show respect by avoiding clothes that may offend, learning about any local traditions, and sometimes adopting modest attire to support student comfort and inclusion. Subtle expressions of personal background or celebration, such as patterned scarves or pins, can honor both community expectations and individuality when chosen thoughtfully.

With creativity and practical planning — even while working with a limited budget — teachers can meet professional dress expectations. A strong foundation in appropriate attire creates space for teachers to discover personal touches and authentic style, setting the stage for blending confidence with individuality in every lesson.

Integrating Individuality and Expertise

Personal Expression, Grooming, Real-Life Insights, and Supportive Resources

Making thoughtful choices about what to wear helps teachers set a positive tone from the moment they enter a room. Many new teachers start with a few basic guidelines: stick with neutral or solid colors, choose clean lines, and keep accessories simple. Over time, teachers can experiment with subtle elements of personal style. Colorful scarves, ties, or statement necklaces can brighten up a basic shirt or sweater without drawing too much attention. A favorite pin or patterned socks might become a signature detail. The key is to look at each item and ask whether it supports focus and respect in the classroom. If a shoe's color is lively but the style remains comfortable and practical, it can showcase personality while staying teaching-ready. But a distracting print, noisy jewelry, or graphic t-shirt could shift the focus away from learning or signal a casual attitude that does not fit every moment.

Matching clothing to the day's needs is part of the ongoing process. A school might have spirit days or themed dress-downs, offering space for more flair. On a parent-teacher conference day, many educators swap out jeans for dress pants or a blazer, signaling heightened professionalism. Even small choices make a difference: classic sneakers in good repair can be acceptable, while battered or flashy shoes might cross a line. One fourth-grade teacher recalls her first open house: "I wore a bright dress that I loved, but later realized the pattern made it hard for parents to pay attention to what I was saying. Now I opt for softer colors and let a scarf or brooch show some personality."

Footwear deserves extra attention because teachers spend hours standing and walking. Supportive shoes — loafers, flats, low-heeled boots, or smart sneakers — keep feet comfortable and help maintain a neat appearance. Sturdy soles and quality materials go further than trend-driven options that might look stylish but leave you achy or distracted by midday. Changing shoes after school, or keeping backup options at work, adds flexibility for anyone who moves between classrooms or runs after students on the playground.

Grooming plays a direct role in presenting oneself as reliable and approachable. Clean hair, trimmed nails, brushed teeth, and clothes that are free of wrinkles or stains help shape how students and colleagues respond. Many teachers develop morning routines that make these steps second nature — setting out outfits the night before or investing in a garment steamer for stubborn wrinkles. Less can be more with fragrance, especially in shared spaces, so opting for unscented or very light scents is a sign of respect for others' sensitivities. Face and body piercings, tattoos, or dramatic hairstyles are increasingly common, yet these details are best considered in light of school culture and policy. Checking in with mentors or administrators about existing norms provides guidance and avoids surprises.

Seeing how choices affect the classroom brings these practices to life.

For example, Ms. Lopez, a first-year high school science teacher, once wore athletic leggings and a hoodie on a day when a district supervisor visited unexpectedly. "I spent all day nervous that I wasn't presenting myself as a serious educator. After that, I found a few comfortable dresses and kept a cardigan in my desk for quick upgrades." Mr. Chen, a veteran fifth-grade teacher, has a ritual: he lays out his clothes every Sunday, choosing simple button-down shirts in school colors, dark jeans (on casual days), and shoes that can handle a fast paced day. He adds small pins related to his hobbies and says, "That's how my students get to know I'm more than just their teacher, but they still know I care about my job."

A solid starting wardrobe for teachers covers needs for busy weeks and special occasions without breaking the bank. Here is a checklist that can help:

- Neutral cardigans or blazers
- Comfortable dress pants or chinos
- Skirts or dresses that hit at or below the knee
- Simple shirts or blouses in solid or muted tones
- Supportive, closed-toe shoes
- One set of more formal clothing for special events
- A few tasteful accessories (scarves, pins, or ties)

For buying on a budget, local thrift shops and online resale sites offer professional finds at friendly prices. Chains such as Uniqlo, Target, or Old Navy carry staples, while retailers with educator discounts like J.Crew, Madewell, or Kohl's can help teachers stretch their budget further.

Reflective questions support teachers as their style evolves:

Self-Assessment Guide

- Does this outfit help me feel comfortable, confident, and ready to lead?
- Would I feel prepared for an unscheduled meeting with a parent or administrator?
- Am I presenting myself in a way that invites respect and attention from students?

Building a wardrobe and grooming routine does not happen overnight. Over the school year, teachers can adjust their approach in response to feedback and changing needs. Wearing clothing that fits well, keeping shoes clean and comfortable, and practicing regular grooming all send the message that the classroom is a place of care and belonging. Professional appearance is part of a teacher's toolkit for fostering trust and building connections, helping every lesson start on strong, positive ground.

Bringing It All Together

Now that we understand the important role professional appearance plays in teaching, new educators can confidently build wardrobes and routines that help them feel prepared and respected. By choosing clothes that fit well, match their school's culture, and balance comfort with style, teachers set the stage for positive connections with students, families, and colleagues. As you grow in your career, remember that small details like clean shoes, thoughtful accessories, and grooming habits speak volumes about your dedication. With practice and attention to these choices, you'll create an authentic look that supports your professionalism while letting your unique personality shine through every day in the classroom.

Chapter 11:
Certified and Empowered: Owning Your Role as a Professional Educator

Leveraging Educator Certification: Standing Out and Thriving in Your Career

Have you ever wondered how some teachers seem to shine in their careers, stepping confidently into leadership roles and making a real difference in their schools and communities? What sets them apart from others who simply go through the motions day after day? Maybe you've thought about how certification could open doors for you but aren't sure exactly what that looks like in practice. If you're thinking about becoming a teacher, switching careers, or preparing for your certification exams, you might be asking: How can I use my certification not just to get a foot in the door but to truly stand out and grow? How do educators balance all the demands of teaching while still feeling fulfilled and making a lasting impact? These questions are common, and finding clear answers can make all the difference. As you move forward, understanding how to leverage your certification thoughtfully will be key to building a satisfying and successful teaching career.

Building Professional Reputation and Leadership Capacity

Building a strong professional reputation as an educator starts with consistent, high-quality daily practice in the classroom. When colleagues and administrators see a teacher creating innovative lesson plans that genuinely engage students — or integrating technology thoughtfully to enhance learning — they notice someone who is both passionate and effective. Educators can further earn respect by maintaining organized documentation systems, such as clear grading records, detailed student progress notes, and accessible curriculum maps. This organization demonstrates reliability and readiness, making it easier for others to trust and collaborate with them.

Meeting deadlines, whether for report cards, data submissions, or parent communications, is another important habit. It signals professionalism and respect for others' time. When peers know they can depend on someone to follow through, it builds a sense of trust and dependability. Demonstrating expertise can also mean presenting a lesson that uniquely connects academic content to students' lives — like linking a math concept to real-world budgeting or inviting community professionals into the classroom. These actions make an educator stand out as both skilled and innovative (University of San Diego, 2022).

Participating in professional development is one of the most strategic moves an educator can make to boost credibility and effectiveness. Workshop attendance, particularly in areas that match personal interest or address schoolwide needs, keeps skills sharp and shows a commitment to growth. Continuing education — pursuing certifications in areas such as ESL, special education, or instructional coaching — positions educators for increased responsibilities and future advancement. Joining professional organizations, such as the National Education Association or subject-specific groups, introduces teachers to new ideas, best practices, and a support network beyond their school.

Collaboration lies at the heart of reputation building. Educators who participate in grade-level or departmental team planning bring ideas forward, volunteer to share resources, and provide constructive feedback. Sharing successful materials such as project-based learning units or digital tools improves everyone's teaching and signals a collaborative spirit.

Supporting colleagues as they experiment with new instructional strategies — for example, observing each other's classes and giving helpful feedback — creates a culture of mutual respect and professional generosity.

Educators develop leadership skills by stepping into roles that shape school culture and student success. Taking the lead in mentoring new teachers, for example, is a powerful way to influence the next generation of educators. Weekly check-ins can create a safe space for new teachers to ask questions, reflect on challenges, and celebrate small victories, drawing on research that shows mentoring increases motivation and job satisfaction for both mentor and mentee (Lysfjord & Skarstein, 2024). Setting up classroom observation partnerships allows experienced teachers to model best practices while also learning from their mentees, promoting a two-way flow of knowledge.

Resource sharing systems are another effective mentoring activity. By curating and organizing high-quality lesson plans, videos, and classroom management resources — and making them accessible through shared drives — educators boost their school's collective expertise. These practices demonstrate a willingness to support others and foster strong relationships, building a foundation of trust and respect that supports further leadership opportunities.

Curriculum development offers concrete opportunities for leadership and career growth. Teachers can propose and create cross-disciplinary units, such as integrating history and literature through themed book studies or connecting math and science through real-world engineering challenges. Developing and piloting new assessment tools or updating existing materials ensures that curriculum stays relevant and rigorous, directly impacting student achievement. These projects require initiative, collaboration, and strategic thinking, qualities administrators look for when appointing teachers to instructional leadership roles.

Practical leadership positions, like department chair or grade-level team leader, often come with increased responsibility and influence. These roles might involve leading meetings, coordinating professional development for a group of teachers, or representing the department in policy discussions. Committees — such as those focused on diversity, school climate, or technology integration — also offer a chance to develop leadership skills while shaping schoolwide priorities. Facilitating professional development workshops or in-service sessions allows educators to share their expertise, deepening their own understanding while supporting colleagues' growth (University of San Diego, 2022).

Intentionally seeking out these opportunities sets educators on a pathway toward greater responsibility, autonomy, and visibility. Over time, they develop key "human" leadership skills, such as clear communication, participatory decision-making, and the encouragement of peers — qualities directly linked to increased job satisfaction and positive student outcomes (Lysfjord & Skarstein, 2024). As educators grow into these leadership roles, their influence expands naturally. They gain a stronger voice in school decisions and become trusted advocates for students, colleagues, and the profession as a whole. These strategies not only open doors to career advancement, but also establish a legacy of positive impact that echoes far beyond a single classroom.

Advocacy, Voice, and Achieving Work-Life Balance

Advocacy and Voice

When educators hold certification, they often feel more empowered to speak up and advocate for positive change. One way to use that voice is by joining advisory committees within a school or district. For example, certified teachers might participate in meetings about curriculum improvements, sharing firsthand classroom insights to ensure changes truly benefit students.

Attending school board meetings and submitting comments on new initiatives also gives educators a chance to speak directly to those making decisions. A teacher could present data on classroom needs to advocate for better technology or more learning materials, clearly connecting student achievement to resource allocation.

Educators working for resource equity may offer testimonials about disparities in their school, such as showing how limited access to support staff impacts student performance compared to schools with more robust resources. They can then suggest concrete solutions like reallocating funds for classroom aides or expanding after-school programs. Certified educators frequently join professional organizations, such as state teacher associations, where they network with peers to craft policy proposals. These proposals may help shape local or even state educational policies. For instance, a science teacher might help write policy recommendations to improve science lab safety standards, then present them to district leadership, advocating from a safety and instructional quality perspective.

To ensure their perspectives are heard, educators can form alliances with like-minded colleagues to amplify their message. They might create action committees, submit op-eds to local news outlets, or lead information sessions for parents and community members. These actions make educational issues more visible, helping educators build momentum for change and support from the public and colleagues alike (National Association of Social Workers, 2025).

Work-Life Balance

Successfully navigating the demands of teaching involves setting practical boundaries. Certified educators often define clear boundaries by not checking work email past a set hour or reserving part of their weekends for personal interests and family time. They may also clarify their availability to parents and colleagues, specifying response times for communication, which prevents burnout and maintains professional relationships.

Establishing self-care routines sustains educators across challenging school years. A teacher might dedicate one evening each week to a hobby unrelated to school, such as painting or gardening, to recharge. Regular exercise, adequate sleep, and mindful eating habits also form the bedrock of personal well-being. Some educators keep a simple gratitude journal, noting successes and moments of joy from each school day as a way to stay positive and motivated.

Time management plays a critical role in sustaining excellence. For example, an educator might use a block scheduling method, setting aside specific time each day for lesson planning, grading, and professional development. Breaking large tasks into smaller steps helps prevent feeling overwhelmed; prioritizing three key goals per day can boost productivity. Certified educators often share these strategies with colleagues during professional learning communities, creating a culture of well-being within their schools.

When teachers care for themselves, the benefits extend directly to their students. Research shows that educators who practice boundary-setting and self-care maintain higher energy and engagement in the classroom, leading to improved student outcomes (Gragnano et al., 2020). Modeling work-life balance also encourages students and peers to value well-being, contributing to a healthy school culture.

Respect and Recognition

Certification not only confirms content knowledge and professionalism but elevates trust from others in the school community. For instance, a certified math teacher introducing a new instructional approach is more likely to gain support from administration due to their verified competence. This credibility facilitates collaboration, as colleagues are eager to learn from and share strategies with certified peers.

Building trust with families begins with transparent communication. Certified educators keep families informed about their children's progress, strengths, and needs through ongoing conversations rather than just formal conferences. For example, a teacher might send regular updates on class projects, explain the learning goals in plain language, and be attentive to parent questions. This consistency fosters mutual respect and makes families feel welcome as partners in the educational process.

Recognition from school leaders, students, and parents often follows visible success in the classroom and active engagement in the community. A teacher who coordinates a successful literacy night or leads student groups receives acknowledgment, both formally through awards and informally through community appreciation. This recognition not only boosts morale but reinforces positive professional practices that ripple through the school.

Strong bonds between educators and families directly influence student growth. When families see educators as approachable and highly qualified, they are more likely to trust school recommendations and support student learning at home. These connections create a collaborative environment where student well-being and achievement thrive (Gragnano et al., 2020; National Association of Social Workers, 2025).

By combining advocacy, self-care, and relationship-building, certified educators position themselves as leaders who create positive change, prioritize their well-being, and earn lasting respect in their educational communities.

Job Security, Personal Fulfillment, and Lasting Impact

Certified educators find doors opening to positions that match their interests and ambitions. Moving from classroom teaching to instructional coaching or becoming a curriculum specialist often requires certification as a baseline. School districts actively seek certified teachers to lead advanced classes, coordinate educational programs, or mentor new teachers. School leadership positions, such as department chair or principal, are rarely accessible without the formal validation of skills that comes with certification. With these roles come higher salaries and access to professional networks, giving certified educators a clear edge when seeking promotions.

Contractual stability is another major benefit. Certified educators enjoy stronger job security through binding employment contracts and union protections. These measures offer critical shields against arbitrary dismissals and provide pathways for responding to workplace grievances. States and districts also typically tie salary scales to certification status, meaning certified teachers can anticipate more regular pay increases and better benefits compared to their non-certified peers. For example, a newly certified high school teacher may start at a higher pay grade and receive annual raises, whereas uncertified counterparts may be limited to temporary, lower-paid positions without incremental step-ups. The predictability of employment and salary progression provides peace of mind and practical stability for those starting or advancing their teaching careers (Lifelong Learning and Training Accounts: Helping Workers Adapt and

Succeed in a Changing Economy, 2018).

A certification can lead to unexpected professional growth. Teachers who attain certification often gain access to valuable specialized training and continuing education opportunities. This ongoing learning allows teachers to adapt their practice and stay current with new instructional methods. As districts establish new programs, such as dual-language immersion or technology integration, certified teachers are first in line for these dynamic teaching assignments.

Relocation, whether across districts or state lines, is also simpler since certification serves as recognized proof of skill and ethics. Eastern states often have reciprocity agreements that allow teachers with the proper certification to transfer jobs without repeating coursework or exams. In this way, certification keeps career possibilities fluid, responsive, and robust.

Personal fulfillment is woven throughout the certification journey. The process itself shapes how educators view their students and their daily work. Certification programs encourage teachers to reflect on their values and goals, leading to lessons that extend beyond textbooks. Certified educators report greater ability to plan engaging, inclusive lessons that support diverse learners. In one case, a certified math teacher working with students in a low-income community tailored her instruction to include real-life budgeting exercises. Students responded with higher engagement, and several later credited these lessons for helping them succeed when managing their finances as adults. These moments, made possible by the methods learned through certification, fuel an educator's sense of purpose.

Success stories accumulate as students reach milestones that once seemed distant. An elementary educator certified in reading intervention implemented a targeted phonics program, resulting in struggling readers advancing two grade levels in a single year. This tangible improvement ripples beyond the classroom. Former students who overcame academic challenges often return to thank their teachers, sharing updates about scholarships and careers. The professional confidence these outcomes instill cannot be overstated. Teachers feel empowered to reimagine their classrooms, foster a positive learning environment, and actively contribute to their school's culture.

Certification ensures educators do not remain static. Pursuing new credentials or specialties, such as special education or technology integration, renews passion and energy. Professional development aligned with certification requirements helps teachers build new skills, deepen content knowledge, and experiment with innovative teaching approaches. As teachers gain mastery, they feel more capable and respected by peers and administrators alike. This sense of achievement contributes to personal satisfaction and validates the long hours and dedication that go into teaching.

The rewards of certification reach across decades, establishing a powerful legacy. Certified educators often witness the influence of their work on entire families as siblings or even the children of former students enroll in their classes. Changes that begin in one classroom spread to the community; a certified science teacher who leads student projects on clean energy can influence local attitudes toward sustainability. By mentoring aspiring educators or taking on leadership roles in professional organizations, certified teachers shape teaching standards and inspire others to enter the profession (Legacy and Community Engagement Leads to Impact: How Mickey's Popcorn Prioritizes Work-Based Learning to Grow Their Business, 2025).

Some teachers extend their reach through published curriculum materials, workshops, or district-wide initiatives. The consistent standards upheld by certification allow educators to drive education reforms that improve outcomes for many students. The ripple effect is clear when former students become teachers themselves, cite their mentors as inspiration, and carry forward the values and skills that shaped their own educational journeys. By investing in certification, educators cultivate both immediate rewards and enduring, positive change in the lives they touch.

Bringing It All Together

Now that we understand how certification can open doors to leadership, advocacy, and career growth while supporting personal well-being and job security, educators are better equipped to take charge of their professional journeys with confidence. By embracing the skills and opportunities that come with certification — like building strong relationships, speaking up for change, and balancing work with self-care — teachers not only enhance their own satisfaction but also create lasting, positive effects in their classrooms and communities. Whether you're just starting out, switching careers, or moving through new certification paths, these strategies offer a clear way forward to a rewarding teaching career that makes a real difference for students and beyond.

Conclusion

Building a Successful Teaching Career: Certification and Professional Growth

You have now come to the point where you are at a crossroads in your educational journey. You now have been equipped with the skills and tools you need to be impactful in any classroom you decide to lead. When you responded to the statement, "So you want to teach?" you made the decision to jump in head first because you probably felt that teaching is easy and anyone can do it. You thought that when you started the teacher certification process it would just be another box to check before entering the classroom. You now know that you were so wrong. Earning your teacher certification turned out to be one of the most meaningful parts of this journey. You have learned that this was not just a formality, it was a deep dive into what it truly means to teach. Throughout this journey you have learned to adapt, problem-solve, and connect with students in ways you never expected. Certification marked the moment you shifted from simply learning about teaching to actually living it- handling real challenges, celebrating small wins, and growing alongside your students and colleagues every day. Whether you are just beginning, changing careers, or navigating a new path from another country, know this: becoming a certified teacher is about more that passing a test, It is about becoming someone who is ready for the real, rewarding work of teaching.

Establishing Professionalism: Certification, Purpose, and Mindset

When I began my journey to become an educator, earning my teacher certification felt like the first major milestone — and it was. But now, having completed the process, I can say that certification is much more than just a credential. It's tangible proof that I met rigorous standards designed to ensure student learning, uphold legal requirements, and earn the trust of the public. It didn't just test what I knew — it assessed how well I could use that knowledge in a real classroom. For me, certification signaled a true commitment to the profession and a promise to uphold educational excellence.

To get certified, I had to complete a demanding sequence of coursework, practical training, and exams. Along the way, I gained a deeper understanding of child development, instructional planning, educational psychology, and classroom management. But nothing shaped me more than my time as a student teacher. Working side by side with an experienced mentor, I had the opportunity to lead a classroom, adapt lessons for a range of learners, and create a safe, inclusive environment where students could thrive. That hands-on experience — no textbook could replace it — was the moment I stopped being a student of teaching and started becoming a teacher.

From a legal perspective, certification is essential. Schools and districts require it to ensure that teachers meet minimum professional qualifications. This protects students and maintains the integrity of public education. Knowing that certified educators are in front of students gives parents and communities confidence — and I felt that weight of responsibility when I stepped into my own classroom for the first time.

More than anything, certification builds public trust. When families see that I've met rigorous standards, they're more likely to view me not just as an authority, but as a trusted partner in their child's education. That trust opens the door to better collaboration, stronger communication, and deeper accountability. Certification gave me credibility — and that's something I carry with pride every day.

I've seen firsthand the difference certification makes. As a certified teacher, I've been trained to use proven instructional strategies, manage classroom challenges, and meet students where they are. I can design lessons that reach different learning styles and adjust when things don't go as planned. I've worked hard to earn this role, and I know I'm better equipped to make a lasting impact because of it. The process wasn't easy, but it was absolutely worth it — for me, and for every student I teach.

When someone begins the journey to become an educator, teacher certification is often the first major milestone. Certification is more than an official document — it's tangible proof that an aspiring teacher has reached a standard of competence set to ensure student learning, legal compliance, and public trust. This process evaluates not just what teachers know, but how effectively they use knowledge in a classroom setting. Most importantly, it signals a dedication to the profession and a promise to uphold educational excellence.

Certification means a teacher has completed a rigorous sequence of education, practical training, and exams designed to demonstrate their readiness for the school environment. This process verifies an individual's understanding of child development, subject-area content, educational psychology, instructional planning, and classroom management. Practical teaching, often called student teaching or a practicum, is an essential component. Here, the candidate works closely under an experienced mentor and proves their ability to lead a classroom, adapt lessons for diverse learners, and foster a safe, inclusive learning space (Pottinger, 2024). It's a hands-on test that cannot be replaced by theory alone.

From a legal standpoint, certification is necessary because governments and school districts require educators to meet set qualifications. This prevents unqualified individuals from taking responsibility over children's education. By upholding these regulations, the system guards both student safety and academic integrity (*Five Educators Discuss Teacher Certification Challenges and Changes and How It Impacts Public Schools*, 2019). Parents and communities can rest easier knowing classrooms are led by those trained to create productive, supportive learning experiences.

Public trust is one of the most important pieces of the certification puzzle. When families learn that a teacher has met or exceeded stringent certification requirements, their faith in the school system is strengthened. This trust creates a positive foundation where collaboration, accountability, and communication can flourish. Certification supports credibility. A certified educator enters the classroom with the backing of a recognized authority and the assurance that their skills have been tested and found effective. As a result, they're more likely to gain the respect of both their students and peers.

Consider a classroom led by a certified teacher versus one with an uncertified instructor. The certified teacher has been assessed on their understanding of instructional strategies and can tailor lessons for a range of learning styles and needs. They know how to manage disruptions, encourage critical thinking, and connect lessons to real life. In contrast, an uncertified instructor may struggle with instructional planning, differentiated instruction, or effective classroom management. Over time, this difference impacts not only student achievement, but overall classroom climate and engagement as well (Pottinger, 2024).

Certification requirements also build professional capabilities in concrete ways. For example, aspiring teachers must learn about trauma-informed practices, culturally relevant pedagogy, and effective assessment strategies (*Five Educators Discuss Teacher Certification Challenges and Changes and How It Impacts Public Schools*, 2019). Each requirement supports day-to-day teaching and helps educators respond flexibly to challenges. These standards go beyond the basics; they ensure teachers are prepared to address issues such as student mental health, language diversity, and special education needs.

In real-world settings, the advantages of certification quickly become clear. Certified educators are often preferred for jobs, promoted quicker, and trusted with school leadership roles. They're called to mentor others, serve on committees, or spearhead innovative teaching projects.

Certification is more than an entry ticket — it's a passport to a rewarding, respected career.

For career changers, certification is a structured pathway into education. Many bring unique skills and life experiences, but certification helps them transition by standardizing expectations and building new knowledge specific to teaching. International educators also benefit; while requirements differ from country to country, most education systems require some form of credential to guarantee teacher preparedness.

Two main pathways lead to certification: traditional programs, often completed in university, and alternative certification routes designed for those switching professions or holding degrees in other fields. Both require demonstration of mastery and classroom hours, but alternative paths tend to be more flexible. Regardless of the route, all certified teachers meet the core benchmarks of their profession (*Five Educators Discuss Teacher Certification Challenges and Changes and How It Impacts Public Schools*, 2019).

Certification also shapes professional identity. Preparing for exams and classroom assessments builds confidence and resilience. As teachers realize how much they have grown in skill and understanding, their sense of competence deepens. The requirements reflect professional standards, emphasizing lifelong learning and adaptation.

A successful path through certification begins with embracing high standards — not as hurdles, but as stepping stones toward excellence. When teachers see certification as an opportunity to sharpen their craft and connect their efforts to student success, they adopt a mindset focused on growth and service. Every requirement, lesson plan, and assessment strengthens their toolkit to make an impact. It becomes clear that certification is not only about meeting expectations, but about exceeding them — committing to a career marked by professionalism, pride, and purpose (Pottinger, 2024).

From Theory to Practice: Applying Pedagogical Knowledge in Classrooms

Developing a growth mindset in the classroom shapes how teachers approach every aspect of their job. When educators believe that intelligence and abilities can grow with effort, they model and encourage perseverance in students. For example, during a challenging math unit, a teacher highlights students' progress and celebrates effort, not just correctness. This fosters resilience and curiosity, making students more willing to take academic risks and persist through difficulties (Western Governors University, 2020). Teachers who cultivate a strong sense of purpose often translate that passion into purposeful activities by setting clear class objectives, expressing high expectations, and connecting lessons to real-world contexts. When students see that learning has purpose beyond the classroom, they become more engaged and motivated.

Translating educational theory into classroom practice starts with designing daily lessons that meet students at their developmental stage. A kindergarten teacher, drawing on Piaget's cognitive development theory, chooses activities like sorting objects by size or color to match the concrete operational stage. For older students, lessons might feature abstract thought exercises or open-ended debates. When applying Bloom's Taxonomy, a middle school teacher constructs discussion questions that address various cognitive levels: "What happened in the story?" (remember), "Can you explain the character's choices?" (understand), and "How would you change the ending?" (create). These questions gradually build analytical and critical thinking skills.

Planning lessons with Gardner's theory of multiple intelligences in mind ensures that students with diverse strengths can access and apply new information. For instance, when teaching a science unit on habitats, teachers offer hands-on activities for kinesthetic learners, create habitat dioramas for spatial learners, write descriptive poems for linguistic learners, and incorporate songs about ecosystems for musical learners. This multi-faceted approach increases overall engagement and helps students connect learning to their unique talents (Feder, 2021).

Differentiated instruction rooted in learning style theories creates flexible pathways for student success. When introducing a new math concept, a teacher might provide manipulatives and visual aids for some learners, work through real-world word problems for others, and encourage small group discussions for students who succeed in verbal or social settings. The teacher carefully observes student responses, making real-time adjustments, such as offering alternative assignments or providing scaffolding for students needing extra guidance. Over time, adapting instruction based on observation and feedback becomes second nature.

Real-world scenarios show how reflective practices, like teacher journaling and peer observations, lead to classroom improvement. After a science experiment falls flat, an educator reviews student exit tickets and their own teaching journal, noticing that too few students participated in hands-on tasks. Recognizing this gap, the teacher restructures future lessons to increase student participation and models the scientific process step by step. By consistently assessing the effectiveness of each lesson, teachers close the gap between theory and reality, driving continuous growth (Western Governors University, 2020).

Measuring student engagement and learning outcomes requires both formal and informal tools. Exit slips, where students summarize what they learned at the end of class, provide instant feedback about lesson clarity and highlight areas needing review. Quizzes and project rubrics aligned to lesson objectives ensure the learning targets are met. Digital platforms, such as quick-response polls, also offer real-time snapshots of class understanding. When students seem disengaged, teachers use these results to modify groupings, experiment with different question strategies, or inject enthusiasm with a new game or discussion method.

Personalized learning based on humanism gives students more choices and ownership. A high school English teacher asks students to select from a list of projects — debates, podcasts, or creative writing — to demonstrate understanding of a novel. Regular one-on-one conferences discover students' interests and challenges, ensuring that the learning journey is meaningful to each individual. Promoting student voice and self-reflection encourages independence and nurtures lifelong learning instincts (Feder, 2021).

Collaborative activities tie into social learning theory. In literature circles, students observe how peers interpret texts, discuss different viewpoints, and learn to negotiate group decisions.

Teachers coach students to model respectful listening and constructive feedback, fostering a positive social environment where collaborative skills grow alongside academic knowledge. These classroom experiences prepare students for the teamwork expected in professional life

(Western Governors University, 2020).

Adapting theoretical frameworks to meet diverse needs demands flexibility. When learners need extra support, teachers might use behaviorist strategies by setting clear expectations and rewarding incremental progress. For older students using technology, the principles of connectivism come into play as teachers encourage research using reliable sources, foster collaboration with peers in digital spaces, and teach digital citizenship. Constant reflection and adaptation make theory alive in the classroom, building the confidence and competence teachers need for certification exams and success in their professional journey (Feder, 2021; Western Governors University, 2020).

Mastering Certification Requirements: Preparation and Adaptability

Aspiring teachers begin their journey by understanding the specific academic paths that lead to certification. Most routes start with a bachelor's degree that includes coursework in education theory, classroom management, and subject-specific teaching methods. Some states require degrees directly in education, while others accept non-education bachelor's degrees if followed by a post-baccalaureate teacher preparation program. In both traditional and alternate programs, candidates further develop their knowledge through student-teaching placements, where they apply learning in real classroom environments (Imed Bouchrika, 2025). These placements not only build instructional competence but also help candidates gather essential documentation — like observation logs and assessment samples — for future licensure portfolios.

Certification also relies on passing required assessments. Most states require content knowledge exams and pedagogy tests, such as the Praxis series or state-specific equivalents. These exams often consist of multiple-choice questions, essays, and performance-based tasks. Reviewing test blueprints and past questions allows candidates to familiarize themselves with common structures and subject focus areas. In some jurisdictions, additional performance assessments — like teacher work samples or video-recorded lessons — are required to demonstrate practical teaching skills. Effective candidates make use of open test preparation materials, join study groups, and use subject-specific flashcards to reinforce key concepts ahead of examination dates.

Understanding the variation in state-specific requirements is critical. State agencies such as the New York State Education Department and the Oregon Department of Education each outline annual or cyclical professional development obligations, timelines for renewal, and additional mandates such as background checks or local workshops (Professional Development Requirements by State for Education, 2025). For example, New Jersey requires twenty hours of professional development every calendar year, while states like North Carolina require seventy-five professional development points every five years for renewal (Professional Development Requirements by State for Education, 2025). Review of these guidelines, and keeping updated with any changes, ensures compliance and career continuity.

Organizing a certification timeline helps in managing overlapping steps and meeting deadlines. Candidates create detailed checklists with application submission dates, exam registrations, and practicum milestones. This can also include reminders for transcript requests, obtaining references, and assembling evidence for background checks. Maintaining a digital or paper portfolio with these documents makes it easier to address state audit requests and track progress against requirements.

Choosing the best-fit certification program depends on individual goals and geographic plans. Candidates aiming to teach in multiple states need to investigate reciprocity agreements or multi-state credentials — while those focused on specialized roles, such as special education or secondary STEM fields, should select programs with robust content-area emphasis (Imed Bouchrika, 2025). Early consultation with program advisors or certification offices provides a roadmap of pre-requisites and tailored advice, particularly useful for international educators or career-switchers.

Strategic exam preparation maximizes performance and confidence. Effective approaches include beginning well before the scheduled test, dividing content into manageable study units, and alternating review with practice exams under timed settings. As part of a comprehensive study plan, candidates seek out supplemental webinars, tutoring, and mentorship programs offered by universities and professional organizations.

Documentation supports both initial licensure and future renewal. States may require logs of clinical hours, completed coursework, or evidence of professional development. Keeping digital folders and regularly updating portfolios streamlines this process. Teachers seeking advanced credentials, such as administrative or specialist certificates, build on this habit by adding professional reflections, leadership projects, and evidence of advanced training (Imed Bouchrika, 2025).

Throughout the process, access to support systems is crucial. University advising offices, peer study groups, and online educator communities share insights on local policy shifts and best practices for portfolio development. Many organizations host workshops on exam readiness, job market navigation, and work-life balance for aspiring teachers.

Managing the challenges of certification requires planning and adaptability. Balancing preparation with work, family, or study requires prioritizing and realistic goal-setting. Many candidates distribute certification steps over several months, focusing on the most urgent deadlines first. For those facing financial obstacles, exploring scholarships, loan forgiveness programs, or employer-based tuition assistance can help make the path more affordable (Imed Bouchrika, 2025).

As education policies continue to evolve, staying current remains an ongoing responsibility. Following updates from state education departments, subscribing to regulatory newsletters, and participating in regular professional development ensures compliance. Certification is not a single-step achievement, but a cumulative process — each requirement and strategic choice builds a foundation for sustained teaching excellence and career growth (Professional Development Requirements by State for Education, 2025; Imed Bouchrika, 2025).

Bringing It All Together

Now that you understand how teacher certification is more than just a requirement — it's a journey that builds your skills, mindset, and professional identity — you're better equipped to take the next steps with confidence. Whether you're starting fresh, switching careers, or coming from another country, embracing the process with a clear plan and openness to learning will help you overcome challenges and grow as an educator. Keep focusing on practical experience, stay flexible with changing requirements, and remember that each milestone you reach brings you closer to a rewarding career where you can make a real difference in students' lives. With determination and the right support, certification becomes not just a goal but a meaningful foundation for your success in teaching. Now that you are ready to teach I hope that you have a wonderful time developing the minds of our nations future. So you want to teach, then let the journey begin!

References

Chapter 1

Online Learning College. (n.d.). Online Learning College. https://online-learning-college.com

NEA, (2020 September 14) Code of Ethics for Educators retrieved from https:nea.org/resource-library/code-ethics-educators

EDUCATION CODE CHAPTER 21. EDUCATORS. (2017). Texas.gov. https://statutes.capitol.texas.gov/Docs/ED/htm/ED.21.htm

BOWEN, B., & WILLIAMS, T. (2024). How Do Alternatively and Traditionally Certified Beginning Workforce Development Teachers Feel About Their Preparedness? *The Journal of Technology Studies, 49*(1), 21–31. https://www.jstor.org/stable/48793905

Certified vs Non-Certified Teacher - Main Difference in 2025 | Teachers of Tomorrow. (2025, April 14). Teachers of Tomorrow. https://www.teachersoftomorrow.org/blog/insights/certified-vs-non-certified-teacher-main-difference-in-2025/

Chapter 2

The Classroom Dichotomy: Get Your Copy Today. (2025, March 21). Student-Centered World. https://www.studentcenteredworld.com/dichotomy/

Bardach, L., & Klassen, R. M. (2021). Teacher motivation and student outcomes: Searching for the signal. *Educational Psychologist, 56*(4), 1–15. https://doi.org/10.1080/00461520.2021.1991799

Yeager, D. S., & Dweck, C. S. (2020). What can be learned from growth mindset controversies?

American Psychologist, 75(9), 1269–1284. https://doi.org/10.1037/amp0000794

Ba, K., Johnson, L., Rivera, M., & Chen, S. (2025). *Innovative practices in teacher education*. Academic Press.

Flook, L., Goldberg, S. B., Pinger, L., Bonus, K., & Davidson, R. J. (2013). *Mindfulness for teachers: A pilot study to assess effects on stress, burnout, and teaching efficacy. Mind, Brain, and Education, 7*(3), 182–195

Hidajat, T., Lee, S., Ramirez, P., & Nguyen, K. (2023). *Digital literacy practices among adult learners. Journal of Educational Research, 116*(4), 512–530.

Chapter 3

Carnegie Mellon University. (2019). *Align assessments, objectives, instructional strategies*. Cmu.edu; Carnegie Mellon University. https://www.cmu.edu/teaching/assessment/basics/ alignment.html

McLeod, S. (2025, June 4). *Piaget Cognitive Stages of Development*. Simply Psychology. https://www.simplypsychology.org/piaget.htmlMcLeod, S. (2025). *Constructivism Learning*

Theory & Philosophy of Education. Simply Psychology. https://www.simplypsychology.org/ constructivism.htmlNational University. (2022).

Learning Theories: Theories of Learning in Education. National University. https://www.nu.edu/blog/theories-of-learning/(PDF) Piagetian and Vygotskian

Approaches to Cognitive Development in the Kindergarten Classroom. n.d.).

ResearchGate https://www.researchgate.net/publication/281578915_Piagetian_and_Vygotskian_Approaches_to_Cognitive_Development_in_the_Kindergarten_

ClassroomPoorvu Center for Teaching and Learning. (2021). Formative and Summative Assessments. Yale.edu; Yale University. https://poorvucenter.yale.edu/Formative-Summative-Assessments

Institute, L. P. (2025, July 16). Learning Policy Institute. Retrieved from www.learningpolicyinstitute.org:

Chapter 4

Agency, T. E. (2021, September 20). *Educator Testing.* Tea.texas.gov. https://tea.texas.gov/texas-educators/certification/educator-testing

Agency, T. E. (2023, May 1). *Test Registration and Preparation.* Tea.texas.gov. https://tea.texas.gov/texas-educators/certification/educator-testing/test-registration-and-preparation

Degree Requirements | Advising | College of Education | TTU. (2025). Ttu.edu. https://www.depts.ttu.edu/education/advising/undergraduate/degree_requirements.php

General and Program Specific Requirements for Teaching a Special Subject for Teacher Certification.(2024).New York State Education Department.https://www.nysed.gov/college-university-evaluation/general-and-program-specific-requirements-teaching-special-subject

Strange, L. (2014, March 4). *Routes to Certification.* Missouri Department of Elementary and Secondary Education. https:// dese.mo.gov/educator-quality/certification/routes-certification

TEACH. (2010). *Getting Certified.* @Teachorg. https://www.teach.org

Chapter 5

Goldshaft, B. (2024, December 18). *Mentoring in practicum: supporting student teachers' learning to notice with collaborative observational tools*. Professional Development in Education. https://doi.org/10.1080/19415257.2024.2441837,

Pattison-Meek, J. (2024, June 1). *The unsung heroes of practicum mentorship: Moving toward a triad model inclusive of student voice to support student teachers' professional learning*. Teaching and Teacher Education; Elsevier BV.https://doi.org/10.1016/j.tate.2024.104553iamalcorndev.(2022).

Handbook - Alcorn State University. Alcorn State University. https://www.alcorn.edu/ academics/schools-and-departments/school-of-education-and-psychology/office-of-field-experiences-and-student-teaching/handbook/

Chapter 6

(2025).Nc.gov.https://edocs.deq.nc.gov/WaterResources/DocView.aspx?id=3267444&dbid=0&repo=WaterResources

Agency, T. E. (2023, February 17). *State Performance Plan Indicators*. Tea.texas.gov. https://tea.texas.gov/academics/special-student-populations/special-education/data-and-reports/state-performance-plan-indicators

Agency, T. E. (2021, May 17). *SchoolCounseling*. Tea.texas.gov. https://tea.texas.gov/academics/college-career-and-military-prep/school-counseling

DAAT List. (2017, May 1). Department of Homeland Security. https://www.dhs.gov/terms

DocumentDisplay(PURL)|NSCEP|USEPA.(2016).Epa.gov. https://nepis.epa.gov/Exe/ZyPURL.cgi?Dockey=P101AMXR.TXT

Texas Teacher Certification | State Approved Program. (2024, September 8). Web-Centric ACP. https://www.wcacp.org/texas-teacher-certification/

Chapter 7

Common Teacher Interview Questions and Preparation Tips. (2023, January 23). Soeonline.american.edu. https://soeonline.american.edu/blog/teacher-interview-questions-and-tips/

Chapter 1: High Impact Recruitment Strategies. (n.d.). Teaching Profession Playbook. https://www.teachingplaybook.org/digital/chapter-1-recruitment

Faculty Perceptions of Electronic Portfolios in a Teacher Education Program – CITE Journal. (2016). Citejournal.org. https://citejournal.org/volume-6/issue-4-06/general/faculty-perceptions-of-electronic-portfolios-in-a-teacher-education-program

Portfolios. (n.d.). Bokcenter.harvard.edu. https://bokcenter.harvard.edu/portfolios
Teacher, S.-O. (2024, May 20). *RecruitFront.* RecruitFront. https://www.recruitfront.com/recruitfront-job-seeker-blog/building-a-stand-out-teacher-portfolio

Teaching Portfolio Development | Michael V. Drake Institute for Teaching and Learning. (2024). Osu.edu. https://drakeinstitute.osu.edu/institute-articles/teaching-portfolio-development

Chapter 8

(2025). Renewateachinglicense.com. https://renewateachinglicense.com/member/cart-cat/nh-new-hampshire-ceu-pd-courses

Continuing Education Units (CEUs) – Educator Licensure. (2024). Mdek12.org. https://mdek12.org/licensure/ceus/

NACC - Online Training Center. (2024). Nacctraining.org.

https://www.nacctraining.org/category/continuing+ed

National Board Certification. (2025, February 12). West Virginia Department of Education. https://wvde.us/educator-staff-development/professional-learning-framework/national-board-certification

Professional Development Requirements by State for Education. (2025). Fullmindlearning.com. https://www.fullmindlearning.com/blog/education-professional-development-requirements-state

The Case for National Board Certification: Lived Experiences to Aspire and Sustain National Board Certification - ProQuest. (2022). Proquest.com. https://search.proquest.com/openview/05478a44dd349294cd886542c74015fc/1?pq-origsite=gscholar&cbl=18750&diss=y

Chapter 9

Benefits of Integrating Technology in the Classroom. (2025, March 16). Southeast Missouri State University. https://semo.edu/blog/blog-posts/integrating-technology-in-the-classroom.html

Nayyar, S., & Gupta, K. K. (2024, July 25). *Cyber Security Awareness: Safeguarding the Digital Future in Education.* https://www.researchgate.net/publication/383206159_Cyber_Security_Awareness_Safeguarding_the_Digital_Future_in_Education

Stavermann, K. (2024, November 13). *Online Teacher Professional Development: A Research Synthesis on Effectiveness and Evaluation.* Technology, Knowledge and Learning; Springer Science and Business Media LLC. https://doi.org/10.1007/s10758-024-09792-9

The Policymaker's Guide to Student Data Privacy – Public Interest Privacy Center. (n.d.). https://publicinterestprivacy.org/policymakers-guide-to-student-privacy/

What are impact of AI Integration in educator professional development? | ResearchGate. (2025). ResearchGate. https://www.researchgate.net/post/What_are_impact_of_AI_Integration_in_educator_professional_development

What Is Educational Technology and Why Is It Important? (2022). Molloy University. https://www.molloy.edu/news/what-is-educational-technology

Chapter 10

Gragnano, A., Simbula, S., & Miglioretti, M. (2020, February 1). Work–Life Balance: Weighing the Importance of Work–Family and Work–Health Balance. *International Journal of Environmental Research and Public Health; NCBI.* https://doi.org/10.3390/ijerph17030907

Legacy and Community Engagement Leads to Impact: How Mickey's Popcorn Prioritizes Work-Based Learning to Grow Their Business. (2025, April). Aspen Institute. https://www.aspeninstitute.org/publications/legacy-and-community-engagement-leads-to-impact-how-mickeys-popcorn-prioritizes-work-based-learning-to-grow-their-business/

Lifelong Learning and Training Accounts: Helping Workers Adapt and Succeed in a Changing Economy. (2018, May 24). The Aspen Institute. https://www.aspeninstitute.org/publications/lifelong-learning-and-training-accounts-2018/

Lysfjord, E. M., & Skarstein, S. (2024, November). Empowering Leadership: A Journey of Growth and Insight Through a Mentoring Program for Nurses in Leadership Positions. *Journal of Healthcare Leadership; Informa UK Limited.* https://doi.org/10.2147/jhl.s482087

National Association of Social Workers. (2025). Standards and indicators for cultural competence in social work practice. National Association of Social Workers. https://www.socialworkers.org/Practice/NASW-Practice-Standards-Guidelines/Standards-and-Indicators-for-Cultural-Competence-in-Social-Work-Practice

University of San Diego. (2022, March 21). 10 Strategies for Effective Teacher Professional Development (with Examples). University of San Diego - Professional & Continuing Education. https://pce.sandiego.edu/10-strategies-for-effective-teacher-professional-development-with-examples/

Conclusion

Five Educators Discuss Teacher Certification Challenges and Changes and How It Impacts Public Schools. (2019). FOREST of the RAIN PRODUCTIONS an Educational Affairs Organization. https://www.forestoftherain.net/five-educators-discuss-teacher-certification-challenges-and-changes-and-how-it-impacts-public-schools.htmlFeder, M.

(2021, September 9). *5 educational learning theories and how to apply them.* University of Phoenix. https://www.phoenix.edu/articles/education/educational-learning-theories.html

Imed Bouchrika. (2025, February 26). *Teacher Certification Requirements by State for 2025.* Research.com. https://research.com/careers/teacher-certification-requirements-by-state

Professional Development Requirements by State for Education. (2025). Fullmindlearning.com. https://www.fullmindlearning.com/blog/education-professional-development-requirements-state

Pottinger, E. (2024, April 16). *Why Passion for Teaching Ignites Great Joy*. GCU. https://www.gcu.edu/blog/teaching-school-administration/why-passion-teaching-ignites-joy

Western Governors University. (2020, May 30). *The five educational learning theories*. WGU. https://www.wgu.edu/blog/five-educational-learning-theories2005.html

Appendix

State-by-State Teacher Certification Tests

State	Certification Tests Used
Alabama	Praxis subject, edTPA
Alaska	Praxis content (SAT/ACT/other alternatives allowed)
Arizona	Arizona Educator Proficiency Assessments (AEA/NES)
Arkansas	Praxis PLT, Subject, Foundations of Reading
California	CBEST, CSET, RICA
Colorado	Praxis in some contexts, content exams
Connecticut	Praxis + Foundations of Reading
Delaware	Praxis content, ACTFL for languages
Florida	FTCE (General Knowledge, Professional Ed, Subject Area)
Georgia	Praxis + GACE
Hawaii	Praxis Core, PLT, Subject
Idaho	Praxis content exams
Illinois	ILTS (Illinois Licensure Testing System)
Indiana	Praxis subject exams

Iowa	Approved program may waive tests, otherwise content exams
Kansas	Praxis PLT + Subject
Kentucky	Praxis Core, PLT, Subject
Louisiana	Praxis Core, PLT, Subject (waivers via ACT/ SAT)
Maine	Praxis Core, PLT, Subject
Maryland	Praxis Core, Content, PLT or edTPA/PPAT
Massachusetts	MTEL (Massachusetts Tests for Educator Licensure)
Michigan	MTTC (Michigan Test for Teacher Certification)
Minnesota	MTLE (Minnesota Teacher Licensure Examinations)
Mississippi	Praxis Core, PLT, Subject, Foundations of Reading
Missouri	MEGA (MoGEA + content assessments)
Montana	Praxis content exams
Nebraska	Praxis Core + content exams
Nevada	Praxis Core, PLT, Content exams
New Hampshire	Praxis Core or equivalent + Subject
New Jersey	Praxis Core + content (recently adjusted rules)

New Mexico	Praxis PLT + content exams
New York	NYSTCE (New York State Teacher Certification Exams)
North Carolina	Praxis Core, PLT, Subject, edTPA/PPAT
North Dakota	Praxis content exams
Ohio	OAE (Ohio Assessments for Educators)
Oklahoma	Praxis Core + Subject, OGET/OPTE for some areas
Oregon	ORELA or Praxis depending on area
Pennsylvania	Praxis or PECT/PAPA depending on program
Rhode Island	Praxis content exams + pedagogy
South Carolina	Praxis Core, PLT, Subject
South Dakota	Praxis Core + content
Tennessee	Praxis Core, PLT, Subject, Performance assessments
Texas	TExES (Texas Examinations of Educator Standards)
Utah	Praxis exams
Vermont	Praxis or equivalents
Virginia	VCLA + Praxis content, pedagogy tests
Washington	WEST-B, WEST-E, NES (state-specific)
West Virginia	Praxis Core, Subject, state assessments

Wisconsin	Praxis subject (Core optional)
Wyoming	Praxis exams

State Education Agencies for Teacher Certification (U.S. & D.C.)

Alabama: Alabama State Department of Education – Teacher Certification https://www.alabamaachieves.org/teacher-certification/

Alaska: Alaska Department of Education & Early Development – Teacher Certification https:// education.alaska.gov/teacher-certification

Arizona: Arizona Department of Education – Certification Unit https://www.azed.gov/educator-certification

Arkansas: Arkansas Department of Education – Educator Licensure https://dese.ade.arkansas.gov/Offices/educator-effectiveness/educator-licensure California: California Commission on Teacher Credentialing https://www.ctc.ca.gov/

Colorado: Colorado Department of Education – Educator Licensing https://www.cde.state.co.us/cdeprof

Connecticut: Connecticut State Department of Education – Certification https://portal.ct.gov/ SDE/Certification

Delaware: Delaware Department of Education – Educator Licensure https://education.delaware.gov/educators/certification/

District of Columbia: Office of the State Superintendent of Education (OSSE) – Educator Credentialing https://osse.dc.gov/service/teacher-credentialing

Florida: Florida Department of Education – Educator Certification http://www.fldoe.org/teaching/certification/

Georgia: Georgia Professional Standards Commission https://www.gapsc.com/ Hawaii:

Hawaii Teacher Standards Board https://hawaiiteacherstandardsboard.org/

Idaho: Idaho State Department of Education – Certification https://www.sde.idaho.gov/cert-psc/

Illinois: Illinois State Board of Education – Educator Licensure https://www.isbe.net/Pages/ educator-licensure.aspx

Indiana: Indiana Department of Education – Licensing https://www.in.gov/doe/licensing/

Iowa: Iowa Board of Educational Examiners https://boee.iowa.gov/

Kansas: Kansas State Department of Education – Teacher Licensure https://www.ksde.org/ Agency/Division-of-Learning-Services/Teacher-Licensure-and-Accreditation

Kentucky: Kentucky Education Professional Standards Board http://www.epsb.ky.gov/

Louisiana: Louisiana Department of Education – Educator Certification https:// www.louisianabelieves.com/resources/educator-certification

Maine: Maine Department of Education – Certification https://www.maine.gov/doe/cert

Maryland: Maryland State Department of Education – Certification Branch http:// marylandpublicschools.org/about/Pages/DEE/Certification/index.aspx

Massachusetts: Massachusetts Department of Elementary and Secondary Education – Licensure https://www.doe.mass.edu/licensure/

Michigan: Michigan Department of Education – Office of Educator Excellence https:// www.michigan.gov/mde/0,4615,7-140-5683_14795---,00.html

Minnesota: Minnesota Professional Educator Licensing and Standards Board https://mn.gov/pelsb/

Mississippi: Mississippi Department of Education – Educator Licensure https:// www.mdek12.org/OTL/OTC

Missouri: Missouri Department of Elementary and Secondary Education – Certification https:// dese.mo.gov/educator-quality/certification

Montana: Montana Office of Public Instruction – Educator Licensure https://opi.mt.gov/Educators/Licensure

Nebraska: Nebraska Department of Education – Certification https://www.education.ne.gov/ tcert/

Nevada: Nevada Department of Education – Educator Licensure https://doe.nv.gov/Educator_Licensure/

New Hampshire: New Hampshire Department of Education – Credentialing https://www.education.nh.gov/who-we-are/division-of-educator-support-and-higher-education/bureau-of-educator-credentialing

New Jersey: New Jersey Department of Education – Certification https://www.nj.gov/education/certification/

New Mexico: New Mexico Public Education Department – Licensure https://webnew.ped.state.nm.us/bureaus/licensure/

New York: New York State Education Department – Office of Teaching Initiatives http://www.highered.nysed.gov/tcert/

North Carolina: North Carolina Department of Public Instruction – Licensure https://www.dpi.nc.gov/educators/educators-licensure

North Dakota: North Dakota Education Standards and Practices Board https://www.nd.gov/espb/

Ohio: Ohio Department of Education – Educator Licensure https://education.ohio.gov/Topics/Teaching/Licensure

Oklahoma: Oklahoma State Department of Education – Teacher Certification https://sde.ok.gov/teacher-certification

Oregon: Oregon Teacher Standards and Practices Commission https://www.oregon.gov/tspc/Pages/index.aspx

Pennsylvania: Pennsylvania Department of Education – Certification https://www.education.pa.gov/Educators/Certification/Pages/default.aspx

Rhode Island: Rhode Island Department of Education – Educator Certification https://www.ride.ri.gov/TeachersAdministrators/EducatorCertification.aspx

South Carolina: South Carolina Department of Education – Educator Licensure https://ed.sc.gov/educators/teaching-in-south-carolina/certification/

South Dakota: South Dakota Department of Education – Certification https://doe.sd.gov/certification/

Tennessee: Tennessee Department of Education – Educator Licensure https://www.tn.gov/education/licensing.html

Texas: Texas Education Agency – Educator Certification (SBEC)

https://tea.texas.gov/texas-educators/certification

Utah: Utah State Board of Education – Educator Licensing https://schools.utah.gov/licensing

Vermont: Vermont Agency of Education – Licensing https://education.vermont.gov/student-learning/educator-quality/educator-licensure

Virginia: Virginia Department of Education – Licensure http://www.doe.virginia.gov/teaching/ licensure/index.shtml

Washington: Washington Office of Superintendent of Public Instruction – Certification https:// www.k12.wa.us/certification

West Virginia: West Virginia Department of Education – Certification https://wvde.us/ certification/

Wisconsin: Wisconsin Department of Public Instruction – Licensing https://dpi.wi.gov/tepdl

Wyoming: Wyoming Professional Teaching Standards Board http://wyomingptsb.com

Made in the USA
Coppell, TX
20 January 2026